START WRITING TODAY!

START WRITING TODAY!

Creative Writing for Beginners

André Jute

DAVID & CHARLES
Newton Abbot   London

British Library Cataloguing in Publication Data
Jute, Andre *1945–*
    Start writing today: creative writing for beginners.
    1. Authorship
    I. Title
    808.02

    ISBN 0-7153-9801-6

Set in 11/12.5pt Sabon by Typesetters (Birmingham) Ltd,
Smethwick, Warley, West Midlands
Printed in Great Britain by Billings & Sons Ltd, Worcester
for David & Charles plc
Brunel House   Newton Abbot   Devon

CONTENTS

1

THE WRITER AND HIS WORK

THE RIGHT FRAME OF MIND

THE successful writer is differentiated from the unsuccessful more by attitude and discipline than by inventiveness or even 'talent'. He* is created a successful writer by the techniques of his process. These techniques are essentially simple matters of self-motivation and craftsmanship: genius as application. Art cannot be taught, and never has been, but almost everyone with the requisite will can be given the tools to turn himself into an artist. This handbook for the writer therefore relates the creative process to practical ways of increasing the quantity, quality, and financial and psychological rewards of the writer's work. The social and commercial background is taken as given; those who wish to change it must either first learn the basic skills of effective communication canvassed in these pages or take up the gun.

Who this book is for The writers to whom this book will be most useful are loosely grouped as creative writers, those who write fiction and non-fiction narratives: novels, short stories; plays, screenplays, teleplays, comic books; children's, junior and teenage stories; biographies, memoirs, travel. Other classes of non-fiction will not be specifically addressed but their writers will of course be able to use much of what is in this book on those communication skills

---

*'He' includes 'she' unless otherwise indicated or impossible in the context.

which keep people reading. Poetry is a condensed form of fiction but depends too much on a unique vision, which in turn dictates form and technique, to be addressed here.

The test of any writing is commercial publication and throughout the underlying assumption will be that I am talking to professional writers, or aspirants willing to make the sacrifices necessary to become regularly published writers.

THREE BARRIERS

A book like this must overcome three hurdles to be of real use to writers.

Perseverance vs talent   The first is that its contribution relative to that of the writer himself is limited by the nature of the physical process of writing.

The thing to grasp most firmly and immediately is that *you can be a published writer if you sincerely want to be a published writer:* becoming a published writer is more a matter of perseverance than of talent. The writers who sincerely want to help themselves are the writers I can help. They already understand and believe that *a writer writes*. A Nobel Laureate told a group of writers standing beside a bar that, within a radius of one mile, there were at least a hundred better writers than any of us; the difference between us as published writers and them as unsung geniuses was only that we had the discipline to write down our great books while the failures merely talked about writing. This is a sobering thought for you as a writer and for anyone putting himself forward as your guide: the best teacher in the world cannot write your book for you, but can only point out obstacles before you reach them or lead you around them once you arrive.

Woody Allen says, 'Eighty per cent of success is turning up.' That's probably true in films, a large-scale but very concentrated team effort. In writing, success comes 98 per cent from turning up at your desk at the appointed time and then actually writing or rewriting for the appointed number of words/hours/months. Yes, months, sometimes years. We're talking heavy perseverance. One per cent of a writer's success probably comes from a god-given skill in communication; despite academic studies to 'prove' the contrary, articulacy has never before been at such a high level or so widespread among the populace at large. Successful writers were not born with some skill in expression or fluency you don't have. They acquired their skill through determined application and so can you. The final one per cent I can help you with, by providing specific learnable techniques to help you solve specific problems that arise for most or many writers, that have arisen for other writers and been solved by them, but which can be debilitating, even incapacitating, when you first meet them without any weapons in hand to combat them.

The mystery of the creative process The second hurdle is that the creative process itself is almost unknown. Note, not 'relatively unknown'. It is virtually unknown. There are very few facts about the creative process that are agreed by the majority of those studying these phenomena and even fewer that will stand rigorous examination by independent scientists from one of the 'hard' disciplines. Anyone offering you a fat book of 'facts' on the creative process is either ignorant or insincere.* Consider how a child learns to speak. Its parents speak to it, it tries a few words and then, miraculously, it breaks into stuctured sentences, an awesome feat. No one has taught it grammar, efforts at vocabulary expansion have been non-existent or intermittent, philologists have not clustered about the crib. Yet the child speaks – and we do not know how the marvel came about. It is such a commonplace that almost no one thinks about it except the professional psychologist. Theories that it must be a genetic mechanism fail to convince many: they feel that's like claiming DNA speaks French in France and has different English accents for

*This is no idle knock. Both as a practitioner of the two 'soft' sciences of economics and psychology and as a practising novelist, I am as keen as anyone for definitive answers.

Boston and Sacramento. Is it important to know why it happened rather than merely that it did? You can bet your advance and your royalties for a big bestseller it is important. If we, as writers, knew the mechanisms by which the power of language arises, we could apply the knowledge to improve our own communication with our readers and be rewarded for our greater expertise in more of whatever coin we seek: self-satisfaction, critical acclaim, greater sales. At the very least, those who try to teach 'style' in creative writing schools would no longer walk on such precarious quicksands.

Or try another example pertinent to our profession: observation, about which nearly as much speculation is spoken and written as about style. Neurologists know everything (or near enough to splice nerves) about the physiological mechanism by which what the eye sees is transmitted to the brain; there is some knowledge, and many soundly based guesses, about how and where in the brain the information is then stored. But here science grinds into low gear. Perception is probably the most studied subject in psychology and, at least by comparison to the baby's sudden outburst into structured sentences, in this field a great deal is known and a huge body of conjecture has earned the respectability of broad general acceptance – if only because no-one has disproved the original hypothesis in the decades since it was promulgated. Yet we cannot account definitively for the variations, as disclosed by differing descriptions, in how you or anyone else perceives an object or, even more difficult, an event. But we need not go into the scientific provenance of the perception of emotions, as implied by an event: suffice it that many psychologists think of Freud as a remarkable and imaginative storyteller but hold him in very low esteem as a scientist. In the field of perception there is today enough solid work to support a whole superstructure of philosophic speculation but it is still a dangerous pastime.

This is where Ruskin's 'creative eye' comes in. Briefly, Ruskin claimed that the artist has a special vision because he has a) the 'innocent eye' given only to the creative spirit and b) belongs to the only caste trained to interpret properly what he sees. His underpinning arguments are not relevant now, nor even particularly interesting, being based on hypotheses of Bishop Beverly which were discredited before Ruskin wrote; what matters is the damage this theory did to our sister-craft of painting, which also illustrates why we are fortunate writing has undergone no such concentrated theoretical foolishness though, as we shall see, the Leavis legacy of shifting the focus of literature from creation to criticism (or, worse, 'analysis'), and the locus of that into the academies, has left us extremely vulnerable to idiocies like structuralism. The tricks of perspective and tone, which had taken millennia to develop to the point where they made realistic painting possible, were easily learned by even modest amateur painters. The 'real' artists who believed in Ruskin's theory, or were taught it by osmosis without possibility of appeal as over the generations it permeated all theory and teaching of painting, could of course not continue to perform tricks even modest amateurs had mastered. They had to be 'different' to prove they had the 'creative eye'. A newcomer then had to prove his 'creative eye' more 'different' than that possessed by yesterday's artist, and soon the outrageous became demodé almost as soon as it appeared. Ruskin, whose theory was conclusively disproved by scientific experiment under controlled conditions earlier in this century, is directly to blame for the philosophical and technical mess in which modern painting and sculpture finds itself.

To restate a point already made, unlike for instance the successful racing driver who differs markedly from everyone else in a multiplicity of measurable characteristics, the successful writer is not psychologically distinguished from the unsuccessful by any significant trait or characteristic except stubborn perseverance at his craft. Writers can claim no special dispensation for their way of seeing or doing things or, in the case of the writer's block, not doing things. It is not their genetic gift of creation that is different, but what they do with it. So all is not lost. Writers interested in helping themselves do better work, or more of it, or gaining more satisfaction from their work, can proceed otherwise than by strictly scientific work or philosophical theorising. We can make empirical observations of successful writers, or of writers we admire for any reason, and attempt, within the bounds of common sense and common decency, to generalise from what we observe. The method may not be statistically or scientifically laudable, but it is all we have – and it works.

In specific terms, much of this book takes the general form: 'This is a problem many writers face. This is how such and such a writer has solved it or how I have solved it. If there are any special circumstances, here they are.' In the chapter *A Writer's Day and Difficulties* we will discuss writers' blocks and their remedies. Painters also have blocks and from my experience as a painter and from talking to many painters, it was impossible not to conclude that the real blocks – that is, not those created by improper preparation or work methods or simple lack of discipline – suffered by painters have the same roots as those which afflict writers. The practical solution of painters' blocks and the practical solution of writers' blocks do however differ markedly and we would learn little from painters that was useful to us as writers in breaking our own blocks, regardless of the self-evident fact that artistic blocks have common roots transcending the artist's precise discipline. However, where experience outside that of writers points to a solution applicable to our own procedures we should not be embarrassed to appropriate it.

Writing as teamwork The third hurdle is that the professional creative process of writing for publication does not take place entirely at the writer's desk or in his mind. A book is a team effort, with the writer, depending on where in his career he has arrived, as either the team leader or the scout of a bunch of publishers, editors, promoters and critics or of their equivalents in films or TV.

Dealings with the rest of the team, and the rest of the world, have an influence on the writer's creative capacity and process and this must be taken into consideration. It is a paradox that one needs sensitivity to succeed at writing, yet the writing profession is one in which the sensitivities are extremely likely to be bruised. The writer needs techniques to protect his psyche or at least to minimise the effect on his work of what novelist and screenwriter William Goldman calls 'the shit endemic to a life in the arts'.

Your unique problems A problem common to all books for writers is that writers, at different stages in their development and career, as they progress, have different problems to solve, or are troubled by different aspects of the eternal problems, and the best solutions also differ. For instance, 'too much plot' mentioned by an editor as a reason for rejection can be devastating for the aspirant writer who doesn't know how to cut (that's in Chapter 7) but will hardly ever happen to the seasoned professional because he would have seen the problem coming before he wrote a word and would have squirrelled away the surplus bits of the plot for another book. Leaving this common problem out of a book for writers is poor service to the novice, who might spend weeks or even months seeking a solution on his own; putting it in irritates the old hand because he has solved the problem so often it no longer holds him up significantly – fifteen minutes or an hour but rarely more than a day – and therefore isn't even recognisably a problem. On the other hand, the novice, overflowing with ideas, will simply stare blankly at a section about recycling old concepts – which the seasoned pro, desperate to keep the flow going for his twentieth or thirtieth book, will pounce on with shouts of glee, certain that right here he will recover the cost of the textbook.

The solution is to split the material into separate books which correspond to the needs of writers at the various stages in their careers. This one aims to help aspirants, novices and newly published writers, those just starting out and with perhaps up to two books published or accepted by a publisher. Writing is itself a learning process – on-the-job

13

training, if you like – and the companion book will reflect this. There is of course no reason the novice should not read that too, if only on the principle that if you know where the curveballs are coming from you can start ducking, or at least brace yourself.

MONEY

It is a commonplace that professional writers talk only of money or money-related subjects (the greedful sloth of agents, the picayune meanness of publishers, the drunken incompetence of the PR department, the rapacious perfidy of film producers, the pathetic lust of directors to share the writing credit and fee) but many unpublished writers ask me about money. The answer is that the diligent author can earn a living and, if he is very lucky as well, become wealthy. However, if one takes into account the 'shit quotient' of a life in the arts, the rewards must be psychological because the financial rewards will never compensate for that; if you can't take the heat, better then to take a safely pensionable job in a computer or insurance company. By way of comparison (and leaving aside painting which I stopped because I became contemptuous of the people who bought my paintings), of the four professions I have practised, advertising and film-making were rat races, certainly, but the odds on success were better than the 4 in 100 chance, at best, of having a first novel published by the first publisher it is offered to, and the financial rewards were high to compensate for the battering the spirit took. In motor racing the rewards were even higher and the chances of success also approximately 4 per cent but the risk was to one's limbs and life rather than one's sensitivities, which makes a fair comparison difficult. In writing the financial rewards are not so high but the psychological satisfactions of creating something worthwhile and lasting more than compensate the real writer for the fact that you need as much determination to succeed as in the other professions I have knowledge of.

HOW TO USE THIS BOOK

This book is intended to be read straight through to familiarise yourself with its scheme and contents, and then to be kept on your desk or worktable where you can refer to it whenever you run into a problem. There is an index at the back for this purpose.

Many seasoned writers are constantly amazed at the positive tone of *thou shalt* and *thou shalt not* found in some how-to books for writers. The writer seeking help should weigh all advice, including that in this book, with his finger in the scales on the side of scepticism. If it works for you, fine. If it doesn't work, you are not the one at fault. There are many ways to skin a cat but in the end always only one skin. This is an intensely personal book, as every book from writer to writer must be until the psychologists can give us firmer guidance. What I am saying is: This worked for me over my twenty-odd books, or for another writer, or works for most writers; there is no reason to believe the solution is particular to one author, therefore it might work for you. Despite the forthright tone, because this would be a dull book if every sentence had to carry the same health warning, these are not the commandments of writing; there never were and never can be any commandments valid in all circumstances. There is no gnostic secret that will turn you into Jacqueline Susann, whose *Valley of the Dolls* was probably the biggest bestseller of all time, or James Joyce, the champion literary darling of our century; they too typed or wrote their books one letter at a time, word by word, sentences strung together to make paragraphs, page by page. In fact, if you feel the need for firm commandments much beyond the beginning of your career as a writer, you are probably not a writer at all, because writing is enjoyed as much as a journey of discovery as anything else.

There is another reason to retain only advice that proves itself by working for you. It is also the reason for giving the practical solution to a problem without analysing the problem too much for fear of being wrong in deducing something from very limited observation. As recently as five years ago I described* the delays writers create before getting down to work – sharpening pencils when they actually use a ballpen, cleaning pipes, repeatedly checking the box to see if the postman has been – as defence mechanisms against that awful moment when they have to write the first word on the blank page. Since then I have discovered that David Higham, the world's leading interior designer and a very busy international businessman, starts his holiday by taking a bowl of water and washing all the picture frames and glass in his vacation home because that helps him relax into his holiday. This rang a bell and led me to wonder if the writer's fidgeting, far from being a distancing and defensive action, is not actually a transition intended to relax him *into* the moment when he can start work. Tolstoy's remarks about the solace of tobacco quite specifically state that this is his interpretation, that his compulsion to smoke is a warning sign that his mind is as yet incapable of writing, rather than merely unwilling. In the awful phrase of Ron, the Nixon mouthpiece, 'Yesterday's statement is no longer operative'. But, if my analysis of the underlying reason for the observed phenomenon is faulty, which may or may not ever be proven, I can stand firmly by the methods offered then to speed the writer into productive work: I know they work for me, for others who have told me so, for writers perfectly strange to me who have written to me through my publishers. Methods which I do not find useful but have often heard others recommend carry a note to that effect and are given with some provenance so that you may judge their value to your own work by their origins. Methods I actively doubt are simply not included because this is not an exhaustive survey; such a thing would be quite as dangerous to the newcomer, and many an experienced journeyman writer, as the professor of creative writing who recommended to novice authors that they use the collected *Paris Review Interviews: Writers at Work* as a

---

*In *Writing A Thriller*, published by St Martin's Press, New York, and A & C Black, London.

shopping list of method and attitude for their own work.

Witchdoctors and other gurus In evaluating any book which purports to help you in creative ventures, you should guard in particular against mystification. The Nobel Laureate whose pertinent remark about what distinguishes a successful writer from an unsuccessful one is quoted above declined to be named on the ground that 'a physician would not share his professional secrets with his clientèle and neither should a writer'. Of course there are imponderables in our trade but they are fewer than the mystifiers would have you believe and much less important than the process of actually sitting down at your desk and starting writing. Remember the motive of the obfuscators and you will not be baffled: the mystique, they think, makes their art 'special', better than yours or mine because their process is invisible and must therefore be awesome – a Ruskinite argument if ever there was one. Witchdoctors are not entitled to respect from sane men. Behind the scenes, if they are any good, which always remains to be judged by their product, they slave and sweat and rewrite the same as the rest of us. Professor John Carey, the most acute of the British critics, answers the more extreme mystifiers by bluntly pointing out that possession of a medical certificate of recent psychiatric disturbance is *not* a guarantee of creativity. We shall ignore the writer who claims, and the critic who agrees, that a piece of prose which is hard to understand or was produced at agonised cost to the writer must therefore be profound; such poseurs are beneath contempt or discussion in a rational book for professionals.

THE PRACTISING WRITER AND THE LITERARY FASHION

Art is not a serendipitous event. It is created only by those who have mastered the technique and craft of their particular discipline. Do not be misled by all the talk of creativity in these pages into believing that we are discussing literature, with or without the capital L.

Literature is a judgement reserved to History, which is not likely to uphold whatever judgements the current academic-literary-critical establishment makes about the competing peers who all adhere to the values accepted by all the judging peers. From Dr Johnson until nearly this century the critics had a good track record in choosing the long-term winners. But since the institutionalisation of criticism in tertiary education the predictive value of lionisation by the official academic-literary-critical establishment has perversely been a virtual guarantee that within thirty years their choice would be unread except sometimes as a prescribed but unloved text in universities. Shakespeare himself, by the values prevalent today, would not be chosen: he acknowledged no 'influence' except Holinshed whom he plagiarised, he worked explicitly for money in a competitive commercial environment, he was immensely popular in his own lifetime, he actively courted the acclaim of the mass and was instantly understood by them because he wrote in the popular vernacular; all these, in a contemporary writer, would offend the academic-literary-critical establishment. John Braine, author of *Room at the Top* and not a man to be deflected by trendy nonsense, observed trenchantly that, while not all bestsellers are classics, all classics are bestsellers. J. B. Priestley noted that all classics are written by storytellers. And I will bet my own modest posterity that John Updike and Irwin Shaw will be read when John Barth, Samuel Beckett and Harold Pinter are footnotes to theses about obfuscation.

However, this book is not intended as the inspiration behind some inferior imitation of Updike or Shaw. The point about a strict attention to the technique and craft of our particular form of expression, and the creative motivations underpinning these techniques and crafts (and, to be brutal, even tricks), is that, once mastered to the extent of thoughtless application, they free you from the possibility of mistake and solecism, liberating your unique expression as a storyteller. Leonardo da Vinci never lectured his apprentices on Art but he ensured that they thoroughly understood the basics of mixing paint, of drawing, perspective and the other mechanics of their discipline – without which they could not ever become artists – as well as the reasons why mastery of technique contributes to communication (but keep in mind our admission that we do not truly know much more about perception than Leonardo did). The modern masters of our craft, narrative prose, often advance the art form by breaking the rules, but they do so meaningfully only because they understand the underlying rationale of the rules; all else is barbaric vandalism inspired by an egotism unsupported by talent or thought.

'Meaningfully' means that the result may be understood by the average man or woman, not just a like-minded minority élite. Jane Austen and Leo Tolstoy do not demand special skills, knowledge or training from the reader to be comprehensible. Anyone, without exception, who cannot make himself understood to the meanest intelligence among registered library card-holders is not a storyteller. In fact, it is hard to discover one great mind, storyteller or not, who did not strive for simplicity and comprehensibility by the largest possible audience. The philosopher Kant bemoaned his inability to express himself simply and wished others would popularise him. The desire for impenetrability by all but an élite stains the pseudo-intellectual quite unmistakably.

On the dangers of 'schools' If you wish to be a storyteller with a chance of immortality, it might be as well for you to understand how a self-appointed priesthood can pervert an art form so that you do not succumb to the blandishments of minority self-election. Above we discussed the century-long Ruskinite anarchism in painting and sculpture but, compared to writing, painting is a peripheral art form. There is no accessible study of the related phenomenon in literature but Paul Johnson has several chapters that are applicable in *Enemies of Society* (Weidenfeld & Nicolson, London); he is also an author generally worth reading for the clarity with which he presents complicated ideas. We all have to live somewhere and that makes architecture, next to television, the most pervasive art form of our time, and it is one which has suffered a clear-cut example of the kind of mischief we are discussing. Tom Wolfe's brief *From Bauhaus to Our House* describes how a bunch of sub-Marxian middle- and upper-class, even aristocratic, refugees imposed their patronising architectural concept of worker-housing, already rejected by the proletariat of their native land, on the corporations and citizens of the richest and most egalitarian nation on earth, the United States. Don't let Wolfe's hilarious style blind you to the tragedy of his tale: genuine creativity and innovation has been stifled in American architecture for more than two generations. Its only remaining outlet is in jokes in the poorest possible taste to be enjoyed only by other initiates of the same professional coterie, like Venturi's huge but non-working gold-anodised TV aerial 'decorating' an old people's home in Phildadelphia because, according to the contemptuous architect, television dominates the lives of the elderly. Instead of laughing, ask yourself if there are not parallel dangers in the modern literary scene, whether you should not examine the validity of assumptions underlying the criteria its establishment holds dear, for instance whether the demand for 'relevance', often unexpressed but none the less present, if acceded to for fashionable approval, will not date your work unbearably in twenty years, or a hundred.

This is not sour grapes. The critics have always treated my work better than it deserved, in many cases extravagantly so, and those few books which have not shared this fortunate fate attracted a public apparently immune to critical opinion who have made them my biggest earners. But no artist worth the name accepts without examination the contemporary assumptions and presumptions of his discipline (for instance the claimed right of intellectuals to prescribe solutions to political problems without ever exposing themselves to the objective public test of running for election).

There is another subject we shall not belabour. This is style, in many minds related to the 'schools' and attitudes discussed above. The reason for not having extensive chapters on aspects of style is that this book and its companion volume are virtually in total about style. That is because your unique style is what remains after all excrescences (mannerisms which interfere with effective communication, obfuscations, structural solecisms, and so on) have been removed from your manuscript: style as an attribute that was present all along but hidden under the excess baggage that results from ignorance, incompetence, or unexamined assumptions about what storytelling entails which in turn create superfluous affectations. Think of a sailing yacht dry-docked. The barnacles have to be removed before the beauty of the keel and the skill of the boatwright may be appreciated. Many schools of creative writing consider style as something tacked on, and proper language ditto by natural extension, but that is simply wrong, as an hour's consideration of any great writer (Austen is good) will promptly convince you; no writer with an off-campus audience believes in 'style' as a separate entity. On language, which with structure is the expression of style, I will have something more to say, but again in reductionist terms – not because I am by persuasion a minimalist (god forbid!)* – but because even the most baroque minds must order and control their output to communicate convincingly with their fellows. Publication, which is large-scale communication, is the acid test. Which is where we started out on getting to know each other.

---

*I am not against minimalist theory in principle, and indeed am temperamentally inclined to appreciate much of its rational technical argument, but agree with Saul Bellow, who has shown in A Theft that he can work intelligibly and effectively in their style, that 'Minimalism is okay if there is some pressure behind the words. The problem is that most minimalists are just – minimal.' A theory is useless if its method utterly consumes the message it is intended to carry; for a writer, the method cannot ever be the message: a rose can be a rose can be a rose can be a rose only once before you have to pass from flora to fauna or go down in literature as an infernal bore. And a school, any school, becomes abhorrent the moment its evangelists reject reason and the cross-fertilisation of compromise for the fanatical absolutism of 'Those who are not totally committed to us are totally against us.' I therefore reserve the right to appropriate the arguments and forms of minimalism, or any other-ism, where they are useful to your or my work, but would be outraged if some lazy commentator classed me with the minimalists or any other-ists. There must be a PhD for some enterprising psychologist of literature in the notion that writers who have realised they will not make the grade, instead of giving up and doing something productive, join a 'school' or found one because they will then at least have the Ruskinite claim to fame of being 'different'.

When you should put this book away In a year or two or three if you are an absolute beginner, and sooner if you have had more practice, you will find that you no longer need this book because you can handle all the problems described in it either with the suggested remedies or with variations you have worked out yourself. At that stage you will be well on the way to becoming a professional writer. You will also have a new set of questions and problems. Then it will be time to move on to the sequel to this book.

2
READER, WRITER, MARKET, READER
NOVEL, GENRE AND CREATIVE NON-FICTION

A LMOST every writer was a writer since the first book he read. After reading that first book, only two questions remained to be answered. Would he persevere and survive to be published? And, What kind of books would he write? We shall return, persistently, to persistence, but the generalisation that writers start as readers is probably the least controversial in this book. If you have this book in your hand and have read this far, it is a stage you have long passed. You want to be a writer, others may have told you as fluent a liar as you should be a writer. I – and perhaps other professional writers – have reassured you that you can be a writer if only you want to be a writer badly enough to sacrifice for it.

HOBBY OR APPRENTICESHIP TO A PROFESSION?

What you have to consider next is the depth of your commitment, which we can conveniently divide into four broad levels.

Do you truly want to be published? One meets many unpublished 'writers' for whom publication would be an unmitigated disaster because it would deprive them of the pleasure of suffering publicly for their 'art'. They are beneath contempt but, if they have bought this book or borrowed it from a library in a jurisdiction where I am entitled to payment under the public lending right, they should proceed straight to Chapter 9, *A Writer's Day and Difficulties*, where they will find plently of fuel to stoke creative angst.

Other professions Do you wish the cachet of calling yourself an author to further some other purpose? I do not condemn such an intellectual aspiration, though the amount of sweat and thought you'll have to expend to be published – and an author is specifically a published writer – is so large that you may as well go the full hog and become a professional writer. If there is some professional reason for wanting a book published with your name on it, for instance that you are a politician of thoughtful mien and your advisors want to consolidate that image ('I can't wait to run against a President who owns more tuxedos than books' – Senator Gary Hart), you should seriously consider either patching up some old speeches, so that they appear to be chapters in a unified book, or having the whole book ghosted, because writing a real book will take more time and cause more frustration than you could possibly imagine. Those who write political books of original thought and passion from conviction rather than for appearances, or their political memoirs (especially if vindictive), do not belong here but with those who write about their hobbies and passions, discussed in the next paragraph but one.

Academics speaking to the masses The caveat about time and frustration is unfortunately also true for the academic, perhaps already much published in his own speciality, who dips in here for tips on writing a popular book. His problem is usually that acquiring the skill that brought him eminence in one field precluded every other sort of endeavour, including some that may at the time have appeared to be leisure activities but are now discovered to be required background for a popular writer. A test was conducted with the manuscript of a novel of mine, *Reverse*

Negative, which had, at that stage, a ferociously complicated plot: 75 people divided into three classes were given two-thirds of the manuscript and asked 'Whodunnit?'. Academics fared worst of all; further investigation showed that it was because they didn't read all that much fiction (even in our skewed sample who had all admitted reading fiction – the general run of academic reads *no* fiction). Executives, including a handful of film people who make their living from judging popular fiction, did next best. But the surprise was that nurses, lower-level teachers without college degrees, shop assistants, and so on, scored best of all in predicting the outcome of a novel that was frankly aimed at the upper intelligentsia. They had the habit of recreational reading and therefore a practised familiarity with the conventions of fiction that even those academics who teach literature seem to lack. Because the writer is created by what he reads, an academic without a pronounced, and indulged, taste for popular literature cannot naturally be a popular writer, no matter where he takes his instruction. That is why so many popular books whose contents derive from academic studies are written by the scholar in conjunction with a collaborator familiar with popular books, often an uncredited editor.

Great passions and good That leaves one incidental writer, the hobbyist who writes a book out of love for his special interest, be it gardening or hot rods. For him, paradoxically, writing is easy, precisely because it is a labour of love. His problems are fewer than those of the other incidental writers, named above, or the professional writers, discussed below; on the other hand, his problems of, for instance, overwriting may be directly related to his passion, and therefore all the more painful to surmount. He is none the less, if he has the least skill, or the sense to get a book like this one and make a start on pruning his manuscript into publishable shape, a writer even busy editors will try to help, because his passion will shine through to readers and that is a rare and very marketable commodity, instantly recognised by acquisitions editors who would remain oblivious to literary talent dancing on their desks. I have a special affinity for these writers, because whenever I have written on my hobbies and special interests I have always run into the same problems, despite all my experience as a professional novelist. A man who can write concisely while in the grip of an overwhelming passion is truly a professional author, even if he writes only one book.

Writing as a hobby Hobbyist writers (as distinct from those who write about their hobbies), who write for their own satisfaction while holding down another job or in retirement, must, if they wish to submit themselves to the only test that matters – publication in print or broadcast – meet the same standards as the rest of us. As there is only one possible objective standard, commercial publication, it is impossible to distinguish any problems specific to a writer who is his own final judge. There is a place for the honest amateur but he cannot ask for special treatment.

The aspirant professional writer All these writers need the skills and techniques we will discuss and probably could not write a publishable book without them or a lot of help, but this book and its companion is specifically designed for those who intend to be professional writers and to earn a substantial or at least growing part of their living at writing.

What is important for you as an aspirant professional is not how much, if anything, you have published already, or where. A piece for your high school courant or company magazine does not require the same standard as *The Times* or *Esquire*, or an operating manual for a machine as a novel for a leading literary publisher. What really matters is your attitude, the strength of your desire to succeed, the sacrifices you are willing to make. Writing is a hard and lonely slog in front of a white wall and there are no easy successes. Every apparently dilettante writer being hugely successful will, on closer investigation, turn out to be a swan: serenely indifferent above the water, paddling madly underneath the surface. But take heart, once your attitude is right, everything else comes with practice rather than from genius

– or it comes from genius for those of us who believe the old adage about 99% perspiration. And the attitude itself is mainly a matter of psyching yourself up to routine and discipline, not a great deal different from psyching yourself up to jog regularly in winter. After that, writing for publication is almost wholly a learned skill.

A BRIEF WORD ABOUT PAYMENT

The professional writer is paid for his work. Publication that meets our test of the dividing line between the aspirant and the professional is commercial publication, in a transaction in which money passes from the publisher to the author in return for his literary product. *A professional writer under no circumstances writes free of charge.* That takes care of vanity publishers, who ask you for money to publish your book. However, the new writer, and many established writers, can gain advantages from working for one particular outlet that does not pay very well.

Auntie, or a visit to the Beeb The largest single market in the world for the short story, and also for the thoughtful short non-fiction piece, is a very high quality broadcast literary magazine that actually pays enough to cover groceries for the writing period with a little something left over for the rent. It is the radio division of the British Broadcasting Corporation, known as 'Auntie' to many British and colonial writers because it has put a little something in the tuckboxes of so many, and as the BBC to everyone else. The BBC's television arm is often a market for subjects and treatments commercial television would not touch, but its main attraction for new writers is that the huge script departments actually read everything that comes in and will often give helpful advice to promising writers who have taken the trouble to present their material in the correct format (as published in their book *Writing for the BBC,* available at public libraries and from bookshops, and the leaflet *BBC Script Requirements,* available from the BBC Television Script Unit direct); it is almost impossible to find a British-born television or film writer anywhere in the world who did not get his start with the BBC. But for the absolute novice, the chief glory of the Beeb is its nearly-all-talk Radio Four and World Service broadcast radio divisions (there is also a market for lovers of or experts in serious music in Radio Three), which are voracious consumers of plays, talks, humour, satire, serials, expertise and opinions on every subject under the sun or above it, games ideas, novels adapted for reading or dramatic playing by the very best actors in the world who regularly appear on BBC radio, short stories at the minimum rate of one per day all year round, and too much more to list here. Despite the fact that competition is keen and that they wade through mountains of submitted material – again, the editors in the separate radio script unit do read everything that arrives in their keenness to discover new writers – the most amazing thing to many is how they manage to keep up such quality year in, year out (the radio in my study is permanently tuned to BBC Radio Four during the day and the World Service at night). The very size of their appetite precludes any kind of editorial prejudice, in fact dictates that excellence can be their only criterion and, furthermore, that variety must be their household god. American readers may not know that the BBC is financed by a licence fee collected by the government, but it makes no difference because the pure size of the operation, plus its traditions of excellence and service to the community (rather than to the abstract of culture), serves the same function as the market does. One can make a good living writing for BBC television and a reasonable subsistence writing for BBC radio – and both are top-grade writing schools that charge no fees except patience and courtesy. Wherever you live, I recommend the BBC to you with all my heart.

THE READER AS WRITER

'I can do better than that' is an honest, honourable, and common reason to become a writer but is suspect as an adult rationalisation. Most readers of this book knew

28

subconsciously that they would one day be writers years before they ever expressed the thought aloud. It is amazingly difficult to meet a writer who is not also a reader, and in virtually every case a reader of books in the same vein as those he writes. Henry James is famous, even among those who do not read him, for decrying fiction as frictionless, but inspection reveals less content in this remark than a modern trades description act would consider fair: James read the Latin and Greek fictionalists voraciously. Modern writers of many persuasions are often quoted as saying they do not read other authors in their genre *while they are writing* – the implication is clear that, released from the fear of stylistic or more deleterious influences creeping in unannounced, they are indeed habitual readers of their peers, betters and competitors. The aphorism that those who have reached the highest public eminence read only detective stories seems quite proven by the fact that so many eminent men, when they turn to writing something light, choose to write detective fiction.

What and how much Chances are that you would not be reading this book unless you have not only decided to be a writer but also what kind of a writer you wish to be. It is still, however, wise to consider your reading in the light of the many months or years you will invest in being a writer before you see a return. What do you read? How much of it?

Let us take an extreme example and say that, if British, you read only Mills & Boon romances, or, if American, only Harlequin romances. Let us say you read them at the rate of two or three a week. It is the premise of this book that with dedication and application you could write a book publishable by these houses. But make no mistake, this genre is created to a ferociously restrictive formula, which would add an additional layer of professional discipline to that required for the physical writing. And, if you read nothing else, you would have to set your stories only in the narrow milieu and period with which you are familiar.

Pull the other one, you say, those books don't demand

much more than a downtown doctor's surgery, and any kind of realistic background of, for instance, the political times, would be a recipe for rejection. That's not quite true. But it raises the point that readers are entitled to your honest best and that they can and will spot insincere writers. Those who write with their tongue in their cheek or who 'write down' hardly ever make even one appearance on lists run by professionals of the Mills & Boon or Harlequin class, and certainly never a second. If you cannot read such books with honest pleasure, you cannot write them. Effectively, if you harbour distaste or contempt for any genre or type of book, you should not waste your time trying to write it, no matter how much money you may think the authors earn; your book will not succeed.

Now address the other difficulty facing Hileigh Hypothetical, our unlikely would-be writer, when he starts writing his book: place and period unknown, except only the here and now of his own environment and time. It might be argued that, though whatever might be learned of geography and history in this class of romance is at best romantic twaddle and at worst subversive of civilisation (and Queenie Leavis did so argue on extremely unsound historical ground), it is what the publishers and readers expect and, therefore, Hileigh Hypothetical can do his research for a book set outside his own time and place in the fiction of his predecessors on these lists. There is a kernel of truth here, as we shall see in the chapter on research, but, without a source of additional information, the resulting book would be thinly unconvincing and certain of rejection.

A reading list please Most aspirant writers read more widely than Hileigh, more widely in fact than they realise until they put their minds to it. A novice biographer, asked what she read, replied, 'Biographies, diaries, you know, the usual sort of thing.' Her library checkout list – an objective bureaucratic record – showed biographies and diaries accounting for a fifth of all the books, but there were also novels of several different types, a book on DIY plumbing, a how-to book on music notation, several books on

30

architecture (half of these were related to a biographical project she is working on, the other half she read because she had newly developed an interest in architecture for its own sake), a whole lot of picture books of cities her biographical subject had never been to, a couple of general histories, a book of mathematical puzzles. This list sounds and is unexceptional; perhaps it is even representative. But if you routinely speak to writers and conversationally ask them what they read you'd believe they read only their competitors plus what is directly relevant as research to their current work. One has to dig deeply or visit their bookshelves to discover the range of interests they seem to acquire quite involuntarily. It is sometimes charged that writers are deliberate outsiders, watchful collectors of human foibles; I don't think so, but will agree that writers are involuntary intellectual magpies of information and people.

Make a written list of every book you have read over the last month. Also papers, magazines, films, television programmes (news, current affairs, documentaries, soaps, other drama), quality radio (BBC3 or 4, PSB), plays or concerts you attended, other public meetings (sports, politics, rock festivals). These, together with your physical and emotional experiences, are your capital, the raw material of any book you might write. That the finished article will appear totally unrelated to any of its parents is the magic that makes you a storyteller rather than a journalist.

The list itself is worthless as a direct input to your work but it demonstrates that you already have a richness of experience not enjoyed by Joe Average. If you don't believe that, ask the head librarian of any large city what percentage of the population are active members of the library, that is, have and *use* library cards. To prepare you for a shock, it is generally accepted in publishing circles that in the developed world (UK, US, Canada, Australia, Europe, Japan) only about 2 per cent of the population ever buy a book, and this includes a large number intended for show or gifts rather than to be read. It is this inordinate wealth of vicarious experience which gives you the sophistication and confidence to want to become a writer yourself. Keep reading. It is an essential part of being a writer, and partly it is essential because it gives you a sense of the world beyond your own here and now. It is unlikely that Hileigh Hypothetical would suffer more than a passing urge to write a book; but, if the urge did not pass, he would soon, somehow, find his way to the library, where he would begin the process of self-education you have already undertaken.

GENRE AND PITCH

Even if you belong to that majority of writers entirely unlimited by considerations of marketing, editorial prejudice, taste or censorship, all of which are discussed in the next chapter, you are still overwhelmed by choices. Suppose you read thrillers and therefore know you want to write thrillers. But you read all kinds of thrillers with more or less equal fascination and you can only write one kind (for now anyway). It is an important choice, because it will tie you to a single project for the next year. Or suppose you want to be a biographer, and have a list of possible subjects covering a widely varying range, from a pop biography to a serious political biography. These projects are mutually exclusive, because you can concentrate on only one at a time.

One way is to look at the market. Whatever is popular now with publishers might still be popular with them when you finish your book a year hence – or the market may have moved on, leaving a glut of similar books on the shelves or forthcoming off the presses. This method is so laden with uncertainties that you should use it only as a last resort or as an additional indicator. The established author can ask his publisher to make a choice from his alternative projects; this is more a way of binding the publisher to the choice, good bad or indifferent, than a guarantee that the publisher's choice will be any better informed than the writer's.

The best advice is to make the choice according to your own reading preferences, without any outside reference, by

Desert Island Roulette if needs be. If you have a list of genres or sub-genres in which you are temperamentally capable of working, or, better still, a list of possible titles, ask yourself, 'If I were shipwrecked on a desert island tomorrow and could have only one book, from which genre would it come, or which one on this list would it be?'

Pitch A closely related question is the level at which you intend to enter the profession. Your first one or two books will type you in many publishers' minds forever, so it pays to enter at as high a level as possible. Suppose you intend to be a specialist in rock'n'roll biography. From wide reading of what is available you will already have concluded that the uncritical rave is the dominant mode, that publishers avid for a saleable name (not yours, the star's) will take a hatchet job as second-best, and that objective biography is reserved for other branches of the trade. You should none the less choose the more difficult writing and selling assignment of the objective biography. Whatever you write first is unlikely to be published in the original draft, so why not use it as a showcase of your best skill? Publishers are not fools; they know that the best hagiographers are first perfectly competent biographers who are also true believers (ask yourself why so many pop biogs are by journalists). Publishers are businessmen who want to be in business next year and the year after, and it simply isn't economic good sense to find a whole new raft of writers every year. So a skilful objective biography is a flag to the publisher that you are a professional rather than a passing ship. You will be a biographer after the fad for popstar books has passed. If right now he wants the easier target of a hagiography, he will tell you so, and let you get on with the alterations on the sound structure of your objective biography. Next year – and this is the point where you will make the transition from novice to professional – and perhaps before your first book is even published, that publisher will be back, as he would not to someone he did not consider a professional, asking if you have any other ideas or offering to commission a book from you on a concept of his. But consider what happens if, for reasons you could not possibly guess or discover, the time for hagiography is past when you turn in your own effort: the publisher sees an unsaleable book that he could, had he wanted it, have commissioned from any journeyman pop journalist, and there is no reason for him to note your professional competence and offer you a chance to change the book or to write something else. Worse, it is human nature for publishers to blame authors for missing the turning of the market when they themselves, with many more, and more immediate, indicators, had not foretold the swing.

There are other reasons for aiming from the very beginning towards the top of your profession.

Stretching your present skills It is a common complaint of the unpublished that publishers have moved the goalposts, that their book is better than so-and-so's book. This notion is mistaken. It is not publishers who have moved the goalposts, but the buying public who have become used to a standard of book that improves visibly in every decade, aided and abetted by professional writers who improve their communication skills with every passing year. Publishers are offered more and better books every year and choose accordingly, and to the novice with a book objectively better than so-and-so's this looks like a conspiracy until it is realised that in the five years or ten years since so-and-so's book was published standards have moved on for the better. Anyone who starts today with the aim of writing for the trash end of the market, not in itself a dishonourable intent, is already doomed because in a year, when the book is offered to a publisher, the market will have moved on, and in two years or thirty months, when it is published, it will compare very poorly indeed.

You have to pitch for the top end of the market because it is the only way to be published. You, and every publisher, know that you won't reach the top of our profession overnight, and in what has become a very hard-headed business you will get few brownie points for trying if you don't succeed, but if you don't try, why do you want to be a writer? Remember that the publisher, while undoubtedly excited about first books and new authors, makes his money from a continuing flow of books from each of his authors. If he sees you trying hard and almost succeeding with your first book, he knows you will develop with experience and/or guidance and be able to keep up with the improving standard of the market, and perhaps in time overtake it and hit him with that megaseller every right-minded publisher dreams about. If you aren't reaching for the peaks, even if your first effort is a near-hit quite near the top, a publisher will argue that a writer who could not work up the enthusiasm to try really hard with his first book is unlikely to improve his batting average with his second and his third – and after that the market will leave him behind. I have sat quite stunned in a publisher's office while he calmly told an agent on the phone that an author who still had a book on the bestseller lists would be amicably released from his contractual option-obligation, to go to another publisher. Noticing my expression, the publisher said, 'He's lackadaisical. That first book of his was a fluke. He'll never do as well again.' In fact, objectively (meaning in my opinion as a reader), this writer's second book was superior to his first, but the publisher turned out to be right, the margin was too small, the market standard had moved on too far in the meantime, and the second book flopped. When last heard of, this author was having little success selling his third book. Running to stand still is a new experience for long-established writers but is not particular to the writing profession, though our other work-conditions are often more pleasant than in some rat-races.

With the critics in perfect agreement It is not only publishers who will judge you for all time on your very first book. In the critical mind you will stand or fall never to rise again with your first effort. This is more basic than critical approbation or otherwise, which is subject to fluctuation and revision, usually downwards, over time. With your first book it is decided for all time whether you are one of that small band of authors worth reviewing or not. A really good first book is also more likely to be chosen by one of the small group of publishers whom the newspapers and other critical media have discovered over time to be superior judges of books, and whose lists therefore receive the lion's share of review space. The argument is circular – some authors are reviewed because they have always been reviewed – but I do get tired of explaining to other writers who want to know why my books are reviewed and theirs are not that it is because my first novel was published simultaneously in London by Secker & Warburg, in New York by W. W. Norton, and in Australia by Hyland House, all known as the kind of 'literary house' book-review editors love, and because by some inexplicable groundswell of opinion my novel came internationally to be considered to be innovative and important.

There is only one writer known to me who moved from the one-line-notice class into the major review class, and that is M. M. Kaye, whose *Far Pavilions* was entirely different from her earlier books. A far more typical case is John le Carré who, even when his earliest (and to some of us, much better) books sold only to a rather restricted public, was given much review space; he is that rare writer, the critics' darling who rose to bestsellerdom, but his case is distinctly less rare than that of Ms Kaye. The point is not that good reviews in themselves sell books – bestsellers are almost universally badly reviewed in the literarily sophisticated media. Good reviews will sell a few hundred or thousand hardcover books to libraries but no-one can make a living from that though many publishers consider predictable library sales a mimimum fallback position in calculating advances, print runs and other practical matters of deep concern to the professional author, and public lending right payments do not arise if your book never reaches a library shelf. Quotable reviews can be used to plug paperback books and that is more profitable. Publishers are keenly attuned to these intangibles but, much more important for the author, notice in the media acts as a psychological reassurance of the soundness of the publisher's decision that you are a worthwhile author who

NOVEL, GENRE AND CREATIVE NON-FICTION

should be published. Publishers, just like humans, appreciate having their taste confirmed as superior. Not to reach out for all the help you can get would be arrogant.

The professional full circle Finally, a consideration you may not appreciate now but that you will understand sooner or later if you become a full-time professional writer: once you have demonstrated your willingness to pitch for the peaks two or three times, you are allowed a slip or two, even a couple of real disasters, without your publisher deserting you, because if he knows you for a trier he will have more confidence in your ability to recover the track than if he thinks you fluked it the first few times. It can make the difference between eating and having to find another job if a publisher is willing to carry you at the old rates for a dud or two until you regain your pace and again start making both of you some money.

THE PROFITS OF POLITICS

We've already seen that the hobbyist's passionate commitment is a valuable asset in any publisher's office. But as a professional writer you would be fortunate to make a living writing solely about your hobby as Dr D. G. Hessayon, the garden expert, does.

Commitment What if your hobby is a hobby-horse, say a political conviction that socialism is the coming resurrection, or a burning desire for clean water from the tap, or a messianic fervour for breast-feeding, but you are by avocation a novelist – should your conviction constantly illuminate your fiction? For the professional writer the response that counts comes from Mrs Joe Average, the majority of readers, and their answer is clear, they're fed up with having the kitchen sink and other people's daft politics thrust down their throats when all they sought was a little entertainment.

It is my contention that whatever passion of the author is not directly relevant to the thrust of the narrative should be ruthlessly expunged from every book but especially from his first; it takes a great deal of experience to achieve the balance between political conviction and entertainment reached by, say, H. G. Wells or Charles Dickens. Passions are like fashions: those that seem profound in one age are risible in the next. Really good books written as little as a quarter-century ago in which this golden rule was not followed already seem intolerably dated. A publisher told me, in response to a casual question about why she had not published more of a writer whose two books amused many when they first appeared some years before, 'He bombards me with books about London in the swinging sixties. He doesn't understand that nobody cares any more about the flower children. I told him to involve himself in current politics. We'll see.' What we saw, after the author had updated his politics, was a new book which was as good as his first two but with as little chance of standing the test of time; only four years later its concerns already seem a little quaint.

The value of relevance Politically inspired writers and critics prattle about 'relevance' or, worse, discuss your work with 'relevance' as the unacknowledged arbiter of its value. Some of our critics do it from ignorance, being so badly educated in the new universities, or so slovenly in their mental habits, that they do not realise that this sub-Marxian analysis is a Stalinist leftover from pre-glasnost/perestroika days. That this search for relevance is absurd can be seen by following Structuralist thought from Orwell's statement that all writing is propaganda (no, only poor writing, and Orwell knew it) to the post-Structuralist claim that the writer does not create the text, the text creates the writer, which is as daft as the auteur theory in films and would be worth as little space were it not for its hardy perenniality in the mental baggage of so many critics and commentators – and writers, for that matter.

Relevance has a place only in the writings of the convinced Marxist already resigned to being read only by like-minded Marxists. It must be chosen consciously and not allowed to slip in by osmosis because it was submerged in the underlying structure of something – usually in the soft sciences – you read or were taught in college. The problem with relevance is that it dates so quickly. It is of course the hallmark of Marxist dialectic that it adapts glibly to the new discoveries or fads of every year and that is precisely what makes it a poor companion for the writer, whose books are set in concrete from the year of their first printing. The writers who survive are those who treat of the larger issues and ignore the fads of the moment.

Note that 'relevance' is picked on only because it is such a large, easy target. The prohibition on intruding your convictions where they are not directly relevant to the job of work you are writing applies equally to conservative politics and conservation politics. They are quite as irrelevant as the other kind. When the *Times Literary Supplement*, reviewing my novel *Sinkhole*, declared that 'Jute's moral and ecological concerns are important', one of my publishers called it the 'kiss of death'. And that was a disaster novel, in which some small concern for the environment is surely justified; the publisher's point was that I had hit the button so hard that the TLS critic perfectly properly personalised his praise, a sure sign that the author had intruded on the objectivity of the narrative. Ouch!

The reader who finishes the narrative of *War and Peace* and plunges straight into the moral discussions Tolstoy appended is bound to feel, even if he is unaware of their hypocrisy (Tolstoy gloried in the wars he fought in), that the emotional catharsis of this greatest of all novels is demeaned by the puerile ruminations of an inconsistent old man. It is a dire warning for the fictionalist and other non-political creative writer to stay clear.

WOMEN, AYATOLLAHS AND OTHER MAJORITIES

Beyond common courtesy, and whatever bow you wish to make to women's rights, remember that many powerful people in publishing houses are women, either in decision-making positions or as the powers behind the apparent throne.

Also, it costs nothing to consider the feelings of other groups, even if only from the viewpoint of your own safety. Far from suggesting that Salman Rushdie might have changed a single word of *The Satanic Verses*, it occurs to one that, if he had considered the total disruption of his comfortably settled life which the Ayatollah's death sentence on him would cause, he might never have written a single word of it. Andrew McCoy, who has been hunted by the thugs of the Bureau of State Security for his novel *The Insurrectionist*, which depicts a black revolution in South Africa, feels that the Rushdie affair has shattered a period of calm, if not tolerance, between writers and those they dare to criticise which had lasted for nearly a decade since Georgi Markov was killed in London by Bulgarian intelligence operatives; he points out that each time another writer gives impetus to the forces of unreason, the stakes are raised – the price on Rushdie's head is five million dollars – and the possibility of escape for the author becomes less. But Mr McCoy still writes books about BOSS and other African problems that are bound to rile governments up and down the continent, Mr Rushdie has intimated he would do it again (though, with his life involuntarily invested in that one book, what else can the poor man say?) and I doubt I would have refrained from writing *Reverse Negative* even if I had known in advance that it would seriously displease two powerful governments. Authors are incorrigible offenders of the status quo. But make sure you understand all the consequences before you wield that most powerful of all weapons, the pen. Consider also that, come the revolution, intellectuals are historically first in the queue for the guillotine.

THE MULTIMEDIA SOCIETY

There is one further environmental factor to consider, which is that we live in a multimedia society. At the most obvious level, you can sell conceptually the same material in different formats to different media. Writers work not only in books and magazines and newspapers, but on the stage and in films and in broadcasting as well, and many producers, directors and presenters, especially of documentaries, are in fact writers first and television people second. Our test of publication would include all these, even if we do not tiresomely spell it out on every page. 'Books' include, except where the context clearly will not permit it, all these methods of publication. Those are markets at least as large as the purely printed book, and on that account alone, never mind their varying artistic possibilities, worth your consideration.

YOUR PLACE IN THE PANTHEON

Every worthwhile advance in literature (as in many other arts) has been brought about by a maverick against all resistance. This has led would-be geniuses with defective thought processes to conclude that breaking the rules is a short cut to immortality and has dropped several once-promising art-forms into a morass of competitive novelty. Jean Cocteau evaluated the truism more appropriately when he advised new authors to take good note of their first reviews and then to cultivate whatever was most vehemently criticised, because that was what was unique and worthwhile about their work. Robert Graves, on the same subject, adds perspective; he advises the new poet to master all the rules of the old poets (and grammar besides!) before he can hope to gain anything from breaking the rules. Graves also throws in a requirement for a sordid love affair, preferably in exotic parts, but in a book to be left around your house we shall not insist on that. My experience and observation is that genius is something that creeps up on you if you do not first destroy your talent with drink, drugs, sex, idleness or an overdose of self-esteem. The process of Truman Capote's self-destruction as a major writer started on that day when at the age of seventeen in a single post he received his first three acceptances from major magazines. Plum Wodehouse, a notably hard worker even in a gallery of grafters such as this book, observed that success creeps up on a writer so slowly that it surprises him. That may be an inescapable condition of our craft.

For the aspirant it is frustrating to be constrained by a set of rules and warnings that breaking the rules without understanding leads to disaster or even destruction of your hopes of publication. I know, I too was an aspirant once. Nobody springs full-fledged into print. All that can be said in consolation is that the harder you work to master the basic rules so that you can apply them in your sleep, the sooner you will find yourself breaking them with reason and to good effect.

When you have finished reading right through this book, you should start writing, with the next page open before you as a security blanket. Good luck.

3
TRANSMUTING REALITY
DISCOVERING YOUR PLOT*
AND CHARACTERS

T HE new writer is often extremely surprised to find the professional, or even the writer with as little as one book written, casting around frantically for an idea. Most writers come to the realisation that they want to write a book with their first idea for a book firmly fixed in their minds and consciously and subconsciously well developed. It is as well to understand the sources of your ideas, not only so that you may be ready to go with your second book the moment you finish your first but also to protect you against possible problems of plagiarism and libel, to mention only the legal traps of working with unexamined ideas.

SOURCES

Study your reading and cultural experience list again. Add to it a list of professional, personal and emotional events and experiences over only the last week. If you are serious about it, the list can become endless. Now destroy the list because it is incriminating evidence you don't want to leave lying around.

Within and without the writer A truth recognised by every editor, dinned into every recruit to a publishing house,

---

*For 'plot', writers other than fictionalists should in this chapter read biographical plan, storyline, arrangement of facts, travel sequence, chronology, whatever defines the structure of their books and contains the characters that will bring them to life.

and welcomed by publishers (who find true novelty a distressingly uncertain commercial companion), is that there are only seven possible plots. There are plenty of variations but all can be reduced by the applications of more or less ingenuity to one of the seven master plots. You are strongly advised to give the books in the library that analyse plots a wide berth – a hardship because some of them are very amusing – for fear of having your inventiveness stifled. The writer is not required to reinvent the wheel, but that freshness of the idea, to you if to no-one else, is one of the main motivators which will keep you going over the long haul of a complete book. It is better if you do not know that the basic idea is, when reduced to academic dialectic, utterly hackneyed.

Your concept, your theme, your plot can at the reduced level be as hackneyed as you like because what will give it freshness for your readers is the people and the action in it, in other words your treatment of it. In all the following chapters, even when they are ostensibly about something else, character will feature largely. But for now, it is enough to observe that you know all your characters already, from books you have read and people you have met and plays you have seen and neighbours in your street and the television news last night – and the processes of your own mind.

Building on perceived reality It is nonsense to say that all an author's characters are projections of his own personality, even in fiction; if it were true, all the best writers would be advanced schizophrenics which is patently not the case. What is true is that the author can build only on what he can see, what he himself has experienced. The biographer who is such a cold fish that he has never loved beyond the bounds of good sense will never write well about the reckless love of his subject for a married, older woman and does well instead to quote extensively from their letters to convey the hopelessness of their passion. Those who have travelled rough roads often find them best described in the words of writers who were as frightened as they were, even

44

if the writers' descriptions are flawed by their fear; the fearless traveller's description, perhaps more technically competent and wide-ranging, leaves one cold, suspecting his intelligence (some people are genuinely too stupid to be frightened).

The writer's experience need not be at first hand but it must be none the less real and immediate to him. If you believe the slanted documentary that all small-town sheriffs are fat men just waiting to paw your girlfriend or wife on some minor traffic infringement, fine, write it like that. If you don't believe the documentary about cannibals in New Guinea, don't put cannibals into the story you set there because your readers will catch you out in your insincerity. The question is, How can readers catch you out when all you do is report the facts you remember from something you saw or heard?

The answer is extremely illuminating: because the writer's reality and objective reality is not the same thing except in very special circumstances (and then only by an act of will), whatever goes into the writer's mind through his eyes and ears and his nose (not coke, just everyday smells you don't even notice) and fingertips and tongue, whether he knows he is gathering the information or not, is transmuted over time, through a process quite unknown to us, into the magic of his distinctive vision. What goes in comes out different, not distorted, not better, not worse, just different. It is not art because it is raw and the writer still has to shape it, and give it context, and refine it, but the start of the process is already lost in memory, irrecoverable, and quite inexplicable. This accounts for even the novice writer giving his readers a heightened sense of the most mundane events and people. That is probably just as well, or we'd all spend our days in the libel courts for describing our neighbours and acquaintances precisely as they are.

John Braine would not write about a time or place or people he had not visited. That is true of many other writers, especially at the start of their careers. Should that influence your choice of setting? That depends on your personality and perhaps on your circumstances. When you are young, discovery is an adventure and that excitement will speak to your audience. But it seems that when writers cross some threshold – the age of forty? – many of them discover that their memory of places and people and habits is a lot more vivid than the reality of renewed visits.

Chapter 8 on research discusses finding out things you don't know, though you must already know you don't know them. Much more interesting are the facts and connections the writer has gathered and subliminally modified so that they emerge with every appearance of being unique.

Universal plots and unique characters There is a universal way of treating every one of the seven major plots but it is easier to say so than to do it. Consider that every major war throws up one key novel, though it is not necessarily written right afterwards. *All Quiet on the Western Front* by Erich Maria Remarque is by general consent the great book of World War I. Remarque struck the prevailing mood *at the time his novel appeared* just right, as after other wars did Tolstoy, Margaret Mitchell, and after the last great war did Deighton, Heller, Jones and Mailer, here given alphabetically because we are still too close to be certain and literary precedence has to be left to history. Even closer to our own time, a strong contender for the key novel about the Vietnam war and what it did to America is James Webb's *A Country Such as This*.

Let's look quickly at a few other fields of literary endeavour. From the Golden Age, does F. Scott Fitzgerald come to mind? Now put up your own candidate for the nostalgia prize; mine is Anton Myrer's moving novel *The Last Convertible* which, in so far as the main action goes, is set in the immediate pre-war years, but is also a tale of gilded youth. And to describe the condition of the English gentleman, do you say Hardy? Well, fine, but Victor Canning has a claim, and he is better on the pain of love by far; in a generation or two, with no disrespect intended to Graham Greene, we should not be surprised to see posterity rate Mr Canning as highly as Mr Greene. And while we are among those who have seriously considered the bogeymen

46

of our time, spies, who bids Le Carré? Thank you sir, but have you considered Charles McCarry? Now, dear reader, put up your own alternative to Dostoyevsky on sin, Pasternak on love, Condon on the absurdity of man's pretences, Gilbert on Churchill, Johnson on modern history, Sharpe for a good laugh on the complications of modern life, Howard Spring for a great weepie, Graves for the erudite novel. Forget for the moment that it is more than a little juvenile to attempt a ranking of writers at this level; just play the game.

This test is personalised to force consideration not only of the writers and their plots, but of their major themes. It would be as well for you to take all the time in the world at this point to reread such classics and favourite modern writers as you consider essential foundation stones of your literary education and ambition. At the very least, sit for a few hours and consider logically your memories of these books, making notes of their salient features.

Don't panic. You are not incapable of selecting such great themes. In fact, the theme does not make the writer great or even competent – the writer makes the theme great. Dostoyevsky, here grandly characterised as 'on sin', is in fact Dostoyevsky on gambling, murder, betrayal, sordid lust, not in themselves despicable themes, or even petty, but certainly less impressive than the unqualified and biblically frightening 'sin'. Dostoyevsky, who is the greatest prose writer of them all, turned pure anarchic violence (destruction for its own sake) into a moral matter simply by the deep feeling he brought to his subject. You could make a similar analysis of my other favourite writers if you wish, but you no doubt have your own favourite writers and would be better employed making your own analysis of their work, for this is not an *in vacuo* academic exercise but, because reading shapes the writer, self-instruction pointedly relevant to your own work.

If it is not the choice of themes that makes the book, and by extension its writer, great, what does? Put another way: take any admittedly great writer and break down his themes far enough to arrive at the lowest common denominator, and he will seem no different from the serious journeyman writer. It is not his theme that distinguishes his work. His involvement with his characters creates their uniqueness, and the consequential involvement of the reader with these unique – and therefore real – characters is what creates universality. It is a paradox, not much helped by the fact that academics fall into the trap of labelling *themes* 'universal' when they are no such thing, when they are the commonplaces of both low and high literature ('Friends', the scriptwriter has Clint Eastwood say in a Dirty Harry movie, 'are like assholes, everyone's got one'), whereas it is the *character* created unique and human who generates his own humanity and therefore universality. Together with the virtues and rewards of perseverance, that is the main theme of this book, the only magic that will get you published again and again.

Too-popular plots There are, however, plots that are too popular and that you should not touch. You will know them essentially by the fact that they are nine-day wonders in the press, if they last that long. Five years ago I warned that the Beirut hostage crisis, then fresh news, was cause not for a host of hostage-thrillers, because most of them would either fail from overheated competition or not be published at all because publisher and public would have had a surfeit, but for a deeper consideration of the hostility between semitic Muslim and semitic Jew, and between Sunni Muslim and Shi'ite Muslim, and between Persian and Arab. The hostage thrillers have come and gone, several are still forlornly going the rounds, and we still await the thoughtful book, which could be a thriller or anything else, which will illuminate these inter-semitic (does anyone need explanation of the Aryan Persian contribution?) squabbles for us.

Here is a more whimsical example, which fills those who didn't live through it or have forgotten it with a delicious horror. In certain Spanish villages on one religious holiday in the year an ass is symbolically pelted with rotten fruit and stale bread and beaten with a feather pillow. One London newspaper got hold of this story and presented it as the donkey being stoned and beaten to death. Soon every other tabloid was in on the act, whipping up the animal-loving Brits to a frenzy of outrage, with publicity-loving members of parliament promising to ask the Prime Minister why the Foreign Office had not yet broken off diplomatic relations with Spain, and why King Juan Carlos was still allowed to visit his cousin the Queen. Public subscriptions were started to buy the poor donkey. Though surely not all their reporters could be so incompetent as not to discover such a simple fact, not one of these newspapers ever told their public that this little act of piety is played out in many Spanish villages: that would have diminished the sympathy for the one, singular, suffering donkey. At the end of two weeks of this nonsense, journalists were flying around Spain in chartered planes, chequebooks at the ready. No fewer than five tabloids all claimed to have bought *the* donkey from *the* infamous village to rescue him from a fate worse than death, and then death. The next day the donkey story was dead and not another word was heard of it ever again. One hopes those newspapers still feed the donkeys they bought to fuel their circulations. Too ludicrous for words? A sick joke to juxtapose this against the concurrent and continuing tragedy of the Lebanon? Of course. But at least two established writers have picked it up, one a writer of farce who will use it for an attack both on the popular press and on religion (that's his genius, attacking religion as well), and the other a writer of popular books on religious matters, who has simply put it in his files to lie there until he can see some way of fitting it into a book. He has a file called 'Religious beliefs of animals' which he says one of these days will become a bestseller. With his track record, we should believe him. Note that neither of these experienced writers is taking the bare events and extrapolating from them. Instead, they have chosen their large issue, suggested by the event, and will use the event, suitably transmogrified, as an illustration.

Of course a newspaper or the television news is a good source of ideas, but every other writer is reading or watching the same news, and fools will rush in. If you see no large issue you can address, as in the example of the farceur above, then look for a sidelight, a small tangential part of the news that you can develop, as the religious populariser above did. Remember, God resides in the details (Mies van der Rohe), for you as much as for Dostoyevsky.

Other writers' work as source material You should be careful that your work, even if fiction, is never based on only one other book (or a single source of any kind); this condition is normally met because as a professional you will naturally check and double-check everything. With that caveat, fiction can be based on any source whatsoever if libel does not enter into consideration. Non-fiction must obviously be based on a wide variety of published sources, or on original research, or contain a good deal of original thought (speculation, conclusions, etc) to be thought of as solely your own work. You can normally quote short extracts from prose and up to eight lines of poetry without permission but with acknowledgement (author, title, publisher) as long as the extract does not represent a substantial part of the whole, which would not be the case with a poem only a page long, and given that your work is not an anthology of extracts, which implies that your purpose in using the extract must be illumination of your own work. If you quote even one line of lyrics that have been set to music, always get permission because music publishers are litigious. If in doubt, take legal advice, available free of charge or for a nominal fee from most author's associations. The most accessible source on copyright in the UK and USA for the author is the up-to-date articles carried in *Writers' & Artists' Yearbook*, published annually by A & C Black of London, and you should read these for your own general information even if you do not have immediate cause to wonder whether you are trespassing on someone else's copyright.

One source of ideas not much mentioned by practising authors, for fear of litigation and ridicule, is the books of their peers. Even a novelist can find the inspiration for a complete novel of his own in a throwaway remark of another novelist, though he is never likely to admit it. Good novels abound in this kind of rich 'byproduct'. You must of course not steal another writer's plot, or his subplots, and most definitely not his characters, but anything else that sets in train a developing idea of your own is fair game, with the restraint that you should use the idea only when it is so well developed that no one but you will ever know its heritage. The idea for my novel *Sinkhole* came to me while idly leafing through a book on rock formations as I waited to go in to dinner; it clicked with news of a hole-in-the-ground disaster and a possible hostage-and-explosives plot my agent had brought me from a demolitions engineer at his flying club that I had dismissed out of hand as too fanciful and too hackneyed. As an exercise, I once wrote down all the ideas for books that came to me while reading a Richard Condon novel: they totalled twenty-nine but that is an unfair example because Mr Condon sparkles with ideas the way other writers throw off dandruff.

There is absolutely no reason you should not use structures developed or perfected by another writer. My overpraised skill with the flashback should really be credited to Jerome Weidman for *The Sound of Bow Bells*, a book I studied with great care after my first solo efforts at the flashback flickered out. Surely Mr Weidman will not begrudge another writer the time saved by referring to his hardwon expertise rather than wasting months on trial and error.

ONLY ONE SERIOUS LEGAL RESTRAINT

There are statutes on the rolls even in civilised countries allowing the authorities to burn witches. They haven't for a good while now and the expectation has grown with some reason that they will not. Similarly with laws on obscenity practised by writers. We cannot be so sanguine about blasphemy laws in a time of growing fundamentalism but where they still stand we can hope that democratic assemblies will strike them rather than let them be applied. Official secrets cases are normally either straightforward treachery or a case of the government trying to apply censorship; it is almost always clear which is which and we will assume the readers of this book do not intend betraying their countries.

Libel   That leaves libel, which is normally a civil matter, though cases for criminal libel are possible and occasionally brought in most English-speaking countries. Libel is the publishing of a slander by printing and distributing or broadcasting it. Writing the slander in a letter and sending it to someone else is publication. The slander, if spoken, and the libel, when published, impute dishonourable thoughts or actions to a person in such a way as to cause him loss, of face or financially, in his profession or community. Justice is done to the libelled person by the courts awarding him recompense for the actual damage suffered, normally determined by a jury – and who knows what might drive them? – plus punitive damages to an amount in some places also decided by the jury, in others by the judge after the jury has declared them meet. No author who has ever defended a charge of libel emerged either richer or younger and it is not difficult to find examples of authors destroyed by both real and frivolous libel suits. There is only one case on record of an author who came away from a libel suit (which he 'won' because only derisory damages were given against him) and turned it into a successful book, and it is not certain that even the resulting bestseller covered the legal costs incurred by the author in his own defence. Not to mention the wasted time, the mental anguish, the lingering suspicion of friends and publishers that where there is smoke...

The author guarantees in his contract with the publisher that his book is free of obscenity, blasphemy and libel. He also warrants to the publisher that he shall be liable for all damages, fines, etc, levied on the publisher and himself, as well as for his own and the publisher's legal costs. If you are ever charged with obscenity or blasphemy, you could probably argue with reason and result that your publishers know more about these things than you do, and should carry half the legal cost of defence for failing to ask you to change the manuscript. With the charge of libel, unless you can prove exhaustive prophylactic measures, your publishers are likely to attempt to save their own skins by throwing you to the prosecution and the jury.

To avoid charges of libel, there are some simple rules to follow. Take all surnames from a gazetteer (the list of town names in the back of an atlas or road map), take all christian names from a book of christian names. If your characters are Americans, give them a middle initial (you need only state it once) that you can later say stands for something different from the name of whoever claims you have stolen his name and libelled him. If you have a phone in the room where you work, keep the phonebook permanently in another room and make sure you have plenty of witnesses to this. (Ludicrous? Of course. But all that keeps a whole fleet of sharks from bringing frivolous libel suits against you is your poverty. Tomorrow you may have a bestseller...). Never, ever, use the name, face or peculiarities of anyone you know (family, friends, workmates) in one of your books unless so heavily disguised by your subconscious even you don't know the source of the character. If you know the source, so do they.

Check all characters' names against voters' registers for the place where the action is set. The telephone book is second best – not everyone has a phone. Check the names of all characters with professions or crafts in the professional registers at your library or by phone with their professional association. 'Hello. Membership records? I'm a writer and I would like to check that you *do not* have anyone called Darius Littelsmith among your members.' If you find a match, change the character's name and start again.

Don't make up telephone and car licence numbers. Their real owners will have a watertight case for defamation of character against you simply because you are a writer and therefore an undesirable bohemian and here you have associated their hitherto good names with yours by using their car or telephone numbers. This is not a joke: the scenario was lipsmackingly described to me by a professor of law at a perfectly reputable Californian university. Tell the phone company and the licensing bureau you are a writer and they will assign you one of the numbers they keep unassigned expressly for this purpose. Don't use your own phone or car number unless you are resigned to having to change it shortly.

If anyone accuses you of libel, be courteous but neither deny nor admit anything until you have taken the advice of your own professional body, whom you must tell the whole truth; their advice may be to make an immediate and full apology regardless of whether you consider yourself right or wrong, or may be to take specialist legal advice.

The only writer I know well enough to ask about it who has been sued for libel won his case and even received his costs; the judge had harsh things to say about his accusers and their lawyers. Yet he was so deeply scarred by the experience that he refuses to talk about it. His wife says, 'Only child-molestation hearings are nastier than libel cases.'

MARKETING AND EDITORIAL RESTRAINTS

Though your reading directs and shapes your writing, consciously or unconsciously, and, in general, you should let it, there are certain limitations of subject for professional writers without independent incomes. The limitations are fewer than you might think, and onerous only to a few writers, but might exclude the whole of their enthusiasm from publication. One example that comes instantly to mind is book-length prose pornography, which has been almost entirely obliterated by video-cassette and picture-book pornography; perhaps as a compensation, soft porn has recently had a revival in paperback. Erotica, the quality sister of pornography, has been killed by the permissive age more than anything else; one wonders if *The Story of O* would today find a publisher willing to bother. (While this book was in proof, I was approached by an American publisher to write 'erotica' for women. Perhaps I was wrong to refuse.) These are examples of limitations to the ambition of only a few writers, but those few utterly obsessed...

DISCOVERING YOUR PLOT AND CHARACTERS

For the majority, restrictions divide into those imposed by the marketing exigencies of books and the received wisdom of the trade, which is a polite way of saying editorial prejudice.

Publishing still seeks Solomon One of the exigencies of marketing books is that nobody knows anything. When you are an important writer, you will no doubt one day ask your agent, either in hope or exasperation, *What the devil does my publisher want?* A publisher, asked this question, will sincerely tell you he wants the best you can do. Your agent, if he is both competent and honest, will tell you the publisher wants no such dangerous and potentially disastrous thing as your best (ye gods, it could be *experimental!*) , that what the publisher really wants is *more of the same* with which he made money before. Commercially, this is a most reasonable attitude. Creatively, it is a disaster. Publishers cannot tell you with any degree of certainty what the public will buy. They therefore publish what they published successfully before, or what their competitors published successfully last month. Like filmmakers who will buy a bestselling novel and then make an entirely different film under the same name because they are paying only for the recognition value of the name, publishers love books by television celebrities because the name guarantees an instant outpouring of love and money by an uncritical public. (Serious writers should not scoff, especially not the ones who ghosted these books.) Very occasionally publishers publish something simply because they like it. What they abhor is the new, the novel, the unique, because that is always in the realm of uncertainty, a condition any serious business tries to avoid or minimise. Publishing is such big business, it has to be serious. This wilful ignorance is responsible for the waves and trends you see in publishing, like Kondratieff cycles in economics. Unfortunately, I can give you a personal example of how these waves can affect an author. In the middle 1980s I had a very thin time of it, not because my books didn't sell or get borrowed from libraries, but because I write novels of suspense for sophisticated readers and adventure stories for men, whereas the 'me-too' wave in publishing was for women's books, glitz, big family sagas, extended fantasies. My commissions dried to a trickle from publishers who personally liked my work. Now the wheel has turned, publishers everywhere are looking out keenly 'especially for male oriented series, preferably ready-made with several books as go-projects because our need is urgent', the superior novel of suspense has survived the glut of secondrate thrillers that threatened to choke the market, and I have five books commissioned with more knocking on the door. In a year or two we will hear horror stories of writers for the women's market sitting idle. This has nothing to do with my talents or theirs as storytellers and everything with a gadarene rush by the big publishers we depend on into 'the marketing realities of our time'. They don't even have the excuse of fashion, because fashion at its root is created by commitment; with a few honourable exceptions, publishers (as distinct from editors) are driven by the cowardice that seeks safety in numbers. Until recently there was the theoretical choice of going to a smaller publisher but they usually couldn't pay the kind of advances the big boys had cunningly enslaved us with, and they are nowadays mostly divisions of the big boys or in imminent danger of becoming such. You might luck into one of the few independent publishers who pay real money but don't count on it; a far better bet, discussed in the chapter on finding your publisher, is discovering an editor at one of the big boys who will lay his job on the line because he loves your book. As the alternative to the market is a state committee telling us what we can write, we have to put up or choose another profession.

Since, in the most profound sense, what you write chooses you, rather than the other way round, there is not much you can do if your first love is on the downwave when you start writing or when you offer your manuscript. First, you will most likely never be able to predict the next wave. The biggest publishers can't, and they are without question extremely competent marketers. Secondly, if you insincerely 'write for a market', you will most assuredly fail in that market, even if you can persuade some napping publisher to bring out your book. But you can try to present your book to the publisher in such a manner that it seems akin to whatever style is on the upwave of fashion. For example, if in the recent surge of women's novels you had completed a story of five hot-rodding brothers who grew up to be international motor racers, you could have presented it as a family saga of men who are real men – with heavy emphasis on the women who tame them amid the glamour of Le Mans and Sebring. A publisher with a schedule to fill might have grabbed gratefully at such a straw. In any event, given the conditions of the time, it would have given you a better chance of having your manuscript read by someone in a position to make an offer than if you had described it in terms of a bunch of oily macho types mechanicking their way to the Brickyard. This is not to advocate that you lie about the contents of your book, merely that you be aware of marketing realities.

Hollywood hates In Hollywood they despise ice stories and sports movies even before they read the script. Stars don't want to go out in the cold and discomfort; stars will insist on doing the sports stunts themselves because it fits their image of themselves, which causes *beeeg* problems with the insurance companies; even with Robert Redford, a ski movie didn't make any money. It doesn't matter whether these 'problems' are more or less insuperable than others producers overcome daily; what matters is that these things are generally believed to be true. Write an ice movie or a sports movie and you start with two strikes against you. My novel *Iditarod* is one of no fewer than three treatments of the eponymous race that has been floating around Hollywood for the last couple of years; many producers have nibbled but all have given the same reasons for not biting: no bankable stars want to freeze for six weeks. Andrew McCoy says he doesn't even bother to offer his novels, set in Africa, in Hollywood: 'If a movie is made in Africa, it will be made by a London-based producer. In Los Angeles they don't read past the word Africa.'

Pols, poofs and pinks Book publishing has similar prohibitions. Books with African settings are hard to sell in New York. Spy stories that depend on Cambridge deviancy are dead in NY and hanging on by a pinky-nail in London. You might flog a political biography in London a lot easier than in New York but a novel that takes politics seriously is unsaleable in New York and nearly so in London. It is no good arguing that Gore Vidal makes a good living writing novels that take politics seriously – you are not Gore Vidal and, more to the point, there are exceptions to every rule. These no-noes and communal prejudices change over time. What is more, they are never shared by all publishers; if you are diligent, you will find one who is more daring or less conventional than the rest.

What the author cannot know The aspirant and novice can read the trade press but the most interesting and useful information is inside the publisher's head and reaches the trade press either never or in the form of results from which you must guess motivations, an uncertain business. Even an author who is keenly interested in the management and motivational aspects of decision-making in publishing can never know all the imponderables. Better by far to expend your energy on making the book you want to write the best of its kind, as we discusssed in the previous chapter.

SEX, VIOLENCE AND CENSORSHIP

There are voluntary restraints on violence, foul language, explicit sex, and so on, practised by authors according to their individual beliefs. A few of the smaller or older family-owned publishers have semi-formal standards about such things and might ask you to change this or that on moral grounds. Do treat them courteously, even if from conviction you refuse to make the change; after all, they are in effect offering to publish the amended manuscript, which they could have rejected merely with a printed slip. You must make your own decision but many authors feel that what would offend these sane and decent middle-class citizens is exactly what would offend book-buyers and library card holders.

Censorship There is nothing useful anyone can say to you about an attempt by your own government to censor or suppress your work. You should take legal advice and accept your own risks or not in the light of your circumstances. When an attempt was made to suppress my spy novel *Reverse Negative*, and copies were illegally confiscated, I simply went ahead and published in New York and Melbourne before London; I never heard another word from the authorities.

Depending on where you are, defying the censorship laws may earn you a slap on the wrist, a conspiratorial giggle, or something much worse. Andrew McCoy tells the hilarious story of how, on the day he was in the Republic of Ireland, he heard Gay Byrne on the radio interview a priest who was a member of the government's censorship committee, asking the man to name a book they had banned. The priest named McCoy's own *Atrocity Week*! McCoy grabbed his camera, elbowed a little old lady out for a cab, shouted 'The biggest bookstore, quick, for a double fare!' and was delivered to the main branch of the country's largest chain of bookstores. He needn't have hurried. He skulked around with his camera for a whole morning, just burning to catch photographic evidence of the actual act of censorship when they removed his book from the shelves, but nothing happened. At last he started talking to the staff and finally the chain's top buyer came to chat to him. The buyer had never heard of the censorship board and looked politely doubtful when Mr McCoy explained what he had heard on the radio. After telephoning the radio station and being assured it was no practical joke, the buyer restocked the shelves with this considered judgement: 'The book's selling, innit?' The Irish are a truly civilised nation.

The publisher as a censor? In the West there are very few authenticated cases of attempted or successful censorship by publishers, for the sufficient reason that it is unnecessary: a publisher rejects your books and does not have to state a reason. You go elsewhere and find another publisher and that's the end of the story. The question of censorship therefore only arises when a publisher has contracted for a book and then, for reasons of content other than those that would be actionable under criminal law for obscenity or libel, decides not to publish. In short, when a publisher goes back on his word for 'moral' justification. Only three cases of this happening are known to me and one is the celebrated Gollancz/Orwell/Warburg scandal half a century old. Of the two cases of recent times, both involving the same publisher, there will be a blow by blow account of one case in another book because the methods used by the author to achieve justice might be of use to seasoned professional writers dealing with recalcitrant publishers. It is, however, such a rare occurrence that it need not concern the novice at all beyond noting that a publisher who has contracted to publish your book has a legal obligation to print and distribute it even if he decides later that he does not really like it; the onus is on him to prove that he refuses his obligation because the book breaks the law.

It might be useful to the aspirant to examine two cases of what could appear to the unpractised eye to be attempted censorship.

The putatively zealous Zionist A publisher suggested quite tactfully that a novel would be publishable if I made it 'less political'. After carefully rereading the manuscript it became clear she could not be referring to the sections set in the Kremlin, because without them the novel collapses. The only other overtly political remarks were made by an Israeli part-time soldier disillusioned with Israel's incessant incursions into Lebanon. When I asked the publisher to be more specific, she backed off. Let us therefore assume, on the flimsiest possible evidence, that she is an ardent Zionist and it was her Zionism the book offended. That she is (possibly) a Zionist I should have discovered up front and not offered her the book at all, except that I never imagined my book would offend even the most zealous Zionist. This, even if our supposition of her politics is perfectly correct, is not an attempt at censorship, but the publisher's right to publish books she likes, books that promote the causes she believes in. She knew, and she knew that I knew, that I could go down the street and get the book published by a publisher who would not even notice that Israel was mentioned in it. We live in a free country and publishers have equal freedom with authors.

A more definite case In the late seventies I decided to write a book on the life and times and influence of John Maynard Keynes, the key economist of our century. I was promptly given messages through economists I knew that in Cambridge I could expect no co-operation. Inside my own publishers an elderly relict of the Bloomsbury crowd pooh-poohed the whole idea to the board. It was delicately conveyed to me that all these nice people didn't want some rough colonial raking over Keynes' homosexual relationships or his somewhat odd marriage to a Russian ballerina, hurting feelings all round. In fact, I planned a novel written from an economist's viewpoint but the literary establishment simply would not believe me. It was ironic that Keynes' brother Sir Geoffrey offered help a lot more readily than either his old students or his old college. In truth, what the King's College closed archive holds on Keynes might barely be of interest to a dirt-digging biographer of impoverished imagination; a malignant novelist can certainly invent better if he is so minded – but I wasn't. In the end my book remained unwritten not because of obstruction – the information I wanted turned out to be 99 per cent in the public prints and the rest I could have invented without risk of contradiction – but because I discovered my metier is a faster-moving kind of novel than those slow sunlit interwar period pieces. But was there attempted censorship? It helps clarity to split the answer. The director at my publisher may sincerely have believed that a foreigner and outsider could not write a good novel on the subject; my own conclusion is that he acted from personal fear of scandalous revelations that I never intended, and it is significant that after his death several other members of the firm apologised to me for this episode and evidently considered it a blemish on his otherwise distinguished career. As for the Cambridge disciples who refused to help me, that is not even attempted censorship, but their right. Their time, experience and knowledge is solely their property and any author can ask of it only as a gift. Even a serious biographer does not have a natural and overbearing right to whatever documents and information it takes his fancy to demand.

4
INTIMATE RELATIONS
CONCEPT, THEME, PLOT
AND CHARACTER

THE novice writer in his mind sees his first book whole, complete, a revelation on the road to Damascus. This is one of the two large inspirations in our craft that do not interfere with the necessary mechanics of writing the book. The other is insight into character, to which we shall come in its place. All other inspirations are either so destructive of the routine that produces publishable books that they should be stamped on, or are small and the result of hard work rather than serendipity. Savour this inspiration of the book whole and complete, a shining thing, because it comes only once in a writer's lifetime at this intensity,* each succeeding experience being progressively diminished by the knowledge gained in earlier books that the vision is a mirage, because books are not written in one gulp, but created piecemeal, with all the cumulative imperfections of each piece detracting synergistically from the finished whole. Resign yourself right now to the fact that, if you are ever 100 per cent pleased with a piece of work any later than one week after you finish it, you will probably not make it as a professional writer. Ask yourself why so many established professionals refuse to reread their own books – some going so far as to bar them from their homes lest temptation

---

*Saul Bellow, nearly fifty years a writer, says of *A Theft* that 'I didn't start working on it. It just arrived . . . a windfall.' He is a naturally ebullient man, and this novella is the turning point to a new format and style for his work, but his recounting lacks the ring of 'Eureka!'; in half a century an intelligent man can learn a lot of hard lessons.

overcome them to pick at old scabs. Professionals of any type are normally perfectionists but a good writer, whose output is subject solely to subjective standards and none more scathing than his own, resides in an elevated class of perfectionism. Another reason to savour that first blazing vision is that it is well to imprint it on your mind as a goal to strive towards for the rest of your life over many, many books.

Much can be learned by the novice who, before reading this book or any like it, attempts to put his vision down on paper in a complete, finished first draft. The reason this cannot be recommended except to those of great strength of character is that it is a searing experience that has put more promising writers off the craft for good than insensitive rejections by publishers ever did. When I started writing professionally fifteen years ago, there were only two good texts available for the aspirant; of one, John Braine's *Writing a Novel*, I was unaware because none of my libraries had a copy, and the other, Brenda Ueland's *If You Want to Write*, while obviously objectively sound for many aspirants, was, and remains to a large extent, temperamentally out of tune with my outlook.* I did it the hard way and nearly gave up; only my pride that I had never given up on anything else kept me going. It would be silly for me to risk the future of a writer who could enrich all our lives by telling you to try it first without help.

---

*I was nonetheless extremely flattered when the 1989 edition of *Novel & Short Story Writer's Market*, the standard reference for fiction writers published by Writer's Digest Books of Cincinnati, anthologised a chapter from my *Writing a Thriller* next to a chapter from her *If You Want to Write*. She is not wrong in her advice, as I do consider many other wouldbe gurus to be, just different. For those who read her book as well as mine, confusion may be evaded by grasping that the important underlying difference between my attitude and hers is that she believes in an objective standard of literature and I believe that literature is the judgement of history. She therefore wishes to guide creativity towards that objective standard as an end in itself, whereas I attempt to guide it to perfection in its own terms (that is, without received or even moral standards, and without reference to hierarchies of genre and other social distinctions of letters dear to academic analysts) within a technical framework that leads to commercial publication because history cannot judge your work unless it is published and, unless you are rewarded for your work, there is a danger you will not produce enough of it to survive. In the end there is less to this difference than meets the eye: we both want to help you write well and lastingly.

THE COMPLEXITY OF WORDS AND IDEAS

If you have already written anything to book-length, no matter whether it was successful or not, you need read the next section, which is a demonstration of the infinite, infernal complexity of words and ideas, only for the asides.

The rich harvest of words and ideas The cliché about a picture being worth ten thousand words is a lie, even for writers with particularly visual imaginations. Recently a literally graphic example of the richesse of prose arose when I had to create a two-page rough of art for a graphic novel. *Gauntlet* started life as a screen treatment for a pilot feature film to herald a tele-series; film and series were never made. With the approval of the commissioning producer the treatment was written as a novella in a style I dubbed Videowrite, which is deliberately flat, aimed at the kind of people who read 'the book of the movie' only if the movie is entirely devoid of intellectual content and the writer has a vocabulary not exceeding two hundred words; the intention was to sneak in ideas by the back door to an audience I had not reached before. So the assumption was that the two-and-a-half pages of text to be illustrated in the graphic double-page spread would be so barren that a good deal of new material would have to be added to fill the allotted graphic space. This turned out to be a risible misconception. First the number of pages of text to be illustrated had to be cut back. Secondly, the eight main panels on the two graphic pages, illustrated overleaf, contained over three hundred separate pieces of art (in the end it had to be stored in a computer), all mentioned or implied in the text, plus of course emotions, etc, which all had to be conveyed somehow. Since the resulting drawing was far too complicated, even when colour (not shown in this book) was used to differentiate layers, and even after some of the explicating text and dialogue was left off because no space remained for blurbs, much of the material had to be moved back so that the two pages of graphic representation in the end illustrated less than a double-spaced page of text, three hundred words at most.

Try this reverse test: write a story about what you can see on my two-page graphic rough. Try to keep it to less than two double-spaced pages. Now try to explain why it is so difficult to keep your tale inside the required length.

Or, if you would rather stick to your own work, take two pages of your own prose and make a list of every single artifact, person, emotion, gesture, and action to be drawn by an artist illustrating it, with terse descriptive notes of appearance as required. The list is almost certain to require more space than the prose you started with.

Trying this exercise with competent, well-textured poetry is also most revealing.

The right words, we are forced to conclude, conjure up ten thousand pictures.

Closures in the reader's mind We do not here have space to go into why this phenomenon arises; wiser men have failed to devise an exhaustive answer. But it is obvious that your prose, or anyone else's, is merely a framework on which the reader hangs a great deal of additional mental baggage, evoked from cultural references you have in common with him plus his own unique personal experience and memory. The universal writer is the one who evokes experience from most readers. Without this involvement you cannot succeed, but that is a tautological statement about which the novice can do little or nothing; we shall give a whole chapter to a practical aspect of the phenomenon which lies much more easily within your control: involving your readers with your characters.

LITERARY BUILDING BRICKS

If we can demonstrate with such ease that the whole is so much more than the sum of the parts for even two pages, we should not be surprised that the whole of a book, three hundred or so typewritten pages, is a daunting prospect. Yet it must be overcome. You must find a way of seeing around the whole to the bricks your present skills can handle.

Handles We know from simply looking at the length of any published book that it was not created in a day or a week or even a month; given the interruptions of the lives of even highly disciplined professional authors, very few books are written at a single creative gulp; Georges Simenon, the creator of Inspector Maigret, is the only author I know of who managed consistently to perform that almost superhuman feat. This creates a practical reason to break your work down into subsidiary goals you can achieve over shorter periods if you are not to become discouraged. We have convinced ourselves, in the exercises above, that even a couple of pages of prose carry the seeds of prohibitive complexity; you cannot be expected to carry that vision of your book whole and pristine in your mind for all the months or years until you have a publishable manuscript. Again, you need smaller pieces.

Write it down We have now finished with large generalities. From now on I will assume that you have read this book through and are referring back to a section for help with your own current work, in other words that you are either ready to start writing or have started writing and are looking for answers to specific problems.

Write everything down. Ideas, fragments, variations on what you have written or decided, everything. Besides these notes being of intrinsic importance for fixing your ideas at a point in time, whereas in your mind they may mutate into something useless without you even noticing, they are practice at the routine of writing, which is almost as important as having ideas in the first instance. Ideas are so much fluff in the bellybutton of the universe until the routine mental and clerical and editorial tasks of the writer, collectively known as 'writing', turn them into a book. Do not worry about writing ideas down too early, before they are mature. These ideas have been in the back of your head, fermenting, for a long time even if you don't know it. Just don't get into the habit of thinking that what you have typed neatly is carved on stone tablets – every word must remain negotiable until the corrected galleys go to press. If you now change the idea, you have a record, and can go back to the first – almost always the right – version when the new version proves to be a golden calf.

Concept, Theme, Plot, Characters

In this book we shall discuss your book at times as if you could physically separate the concept, the themes, the plots and subplots, and the characters from the melting pot. We shall do it only for convenience, for the handle that momentary division of inseparables gives us. Do not be misled into believing that because you hear me or a classroom teacher talking of a 'theme' that it can be sundered from the 'characters' and survive. It has no reality apart from the other components. Yet, paradoxically, one of these inseparable, and therefore presumably equal, components of your book is the greatest of them all.

Why character must be supreme The professional writer and teacher is so practised or learnt this eternal truth about the supremacy of character so long ago that it has become axiomatic. Yet, when the brand-new writer speaks about loved books, character is not necessarily the aspect of the work given prominence. The brand-new writer tells the story of a sweeping conception by the author, of themes that encompass nations and aeons, of earth-shaking events that destroy whole families and are the making of others. Should you be asked to describe *War and Peace*, this is, perfectly understandably and correctly, the framework you will use. We are after all adults, and well educated and steeped in the conventions of literature. But think back to your wonder when you first read it, perhaps when you were a teenager. If you had been asked then, you would have told breathlessly about Prince Andrei's hopeless love, his exploits in battle, a thousand and one things that he or the other characters had done. And that first unsophisticated vision is the true vision. It is also the way that, mechanically, the book was put together: characters doing things, the whole of their doings building into events, the events building into themes illustrating the concept of the whole which years later will still stick in your mind. The honest truth is, we relate to events, whether real or fictional, only in so far as we can identify them with a character with whom we have empathy. A friend of mine once gave nearly three hundred historians a simple association test: She told each of them 'Korea?' on a rising inflection and noted their response, which was one third 'MacArthur', one third 'MASH' (meaning the characters of a zany movie and teleseries popular at that time), nearly another third 'Not my field' (meaning 'it rings no bell with me and I couldn't care less'), and the rest odds and sods which included the names of Korean politicians from specialists in Asian studies. Historians, eh? What about Korea's thousands of years of high culture? What about their fight against Japanese military, cultural and commercial encroachment over the last century? Even professionals, surrounded by other professionals, in a professional frame of mind, personalise events. It is a human trait and one no writer was elected to change.

There are practical reasons for giving character primacy in your thoughts and your work. As we have seen, readers expect it. But you should also know that editors every month see hundreds of perfectly typed, perfectly plotted manuscripts operated by cardboard mannequins, their strings jerkily pulled by some incompetent author. Most they send back after reading only ten pages. A few they publish because they have to publish something. These books disappear pretty soon. (One of my 'literary' hardcover publishers told me to stress to a Literature Board that I was asking for a grant that all my books from the very first were in print, even those which had never been intended for popular markets. A paperback publisher told me he considered it significant – 'worth a bit extra on your advance' – that my books, which he had published as support leads, were still being reprinted long after the lead titles had flown from the backlist and from memory.) What the editor will pounce on gleefully is any novel that has credible, involving characters. The moment you can show promising characters you are a made writer, no matter how wretched the rest of your effort. Every editor, from the rawest to the ones with millions riding on their sayso, knows that gimmicking a lame plot right is a job any technician can handle while creating real characters is something only true writers can do. Creating characters that breathe is creativity with a capital C – and accordingly honoured and rewarded. This applies not only to fiction, but to all kinds of creative narrative including most kinds of factual non-fiction, where the phraseology substitutes 'presenting characters' for 'creating characters' but the meaning is the same. An editor with a biography by an unknown writer before him does not start checking the facts; he reads for involvement with the subject of the biography, to see if the writer has brought the subject alive. Skill in research will, until disproven, be assumed; skill in characterisation must always be proven before any further progress towards a contract can be made. The same applies to history, where the question is usually not What did they decide? because the facts are known or can be discovered, but Why did they make this truly stupid choice? which is obviously a matter of character-observation and analysis as much as of description of events. When you see it like that, there should be no surprise that the editor, who might have no formal education in history, reads for character and interpretation rather than in admiration of the few new facts you may have discovered. Korea? MacArthur!

While keeping in mind the primacy of character for the end product, let us put some handles on your book so we can shove the pieces around a little more conveniently.

The concept One sound reason the vision appears whole is because the writer is a reader. A complete image is also what he hopes to convey to other readers at the end of the book. Summarise any book you think important in one brief sentence without subsidiary clauses. War is evil. The life of a flawed man who nevertheless achieved lasting good for his fellows through little more than his indomitable will (a recent Churchill biography). That is a concept, a word chosen arbitrarily because 'theme' is reserved for something else. Now see if you can summarise your vision of your own book in a single brief sentence.

Reducing the concept to a single sentence without subsidiary clauses is by far the most difficult of your planning tasks. Spend a day or two on it. Ask yourself if your deliberately cramped definition includes your unique vision; this is as important for a work of fiction, which on the face of it must be unique but is not necessarily automatically novel, as it is for non-fiction. Your sentence, as words, is unlikely to be much improved at the end of the day but your mental clarity about what you are attempting will be much greater after this exercise in reduction almost to the point of absurdity.

Themes After the major concept that encompasses all, consider the main themes of your book. These are points that will illustrate your concept, described not as events or happenings, but in the larger philosophical sense. If you plan a popular history of, or a novel set against, the American Civil War from the conceptual standpoint that the tragedy was a result of the failure of communication between brother and brother, it is immediately obvious that you would wish to emphasise, among other illustrations of and contributions to the truth of your conception, that Lincoln's background and his natural sympathies lay with those whom through force of circumstance he had to fight. It should strike even the beginner right here that this method of formulation throws up marvellous possibilities for conflict in the story – write any that occur to you on a separate sheet of paper, because conflict of character and conflict of ideas is of crucial importance to narrative flow and reader bonding with your work. A concept would have a number of such themes which together would illustrate it. Write down all those you can think of; more will probably come to you later, often as late as in writing or rewriting the actual book. It doesn't matter how many themes you have, or how few, as long as the collective impact of these large themes together illustrates your concept. It should be easier

73

to spot holes in your idea when all its main components are written on a single or a few sheets of paper, rather than in a completed book of several hundred pages.

The contrary theme At this stage the historian and biographer and other writers of non-fiction, but the novelist as well in more cases than one would at first think, come across the theme that runs counter to the concept, that seems to disprove it. For god's sake, don't exclude it! Write it down before you forget it! All conflict is grist to the mill. It would be a foolhardy commentator indeed who argued that Tolstoy nowhere glamorises war; no practising writer would even attempt to argue that Tolstoy could have written a better book had he been more consistent (it is in the philosophical appendix that his inconsistency is incongruous, not in the novel); most, indeed, will state as an act of both reason and faith that without the tension of opposites Tolstoy's and every other apparently self-contradictory great novel would collapse. Objective truth, warts and all, is the cornerstone of every book that has survived the toughest critic of all, Father Time. Life itself gains its uncomfortable corners from its internal and external contradictions. Books are representations of life in precisely the way that the best paintings are and the writer who stylises his representation so much that all corners are round and unobtrusive fades into the wallpaper (like so many modern painters do). Abhor or avoid the truth, and you will sink without a ripple.

Taking our War Between the States example a step further, say it comes to you in the planning or the writing that in a civil war there can be no neutrals. A voice behind your ear says that is a cliché. Tell that devil to get lost. Wholly fresh themes are too few and far between to concern yourself with; they will come to you or not as a matter of luck; worry instead about a fresh viewpoint or treatment of universal themes. Ah yes, the voice whispers, but the absence of neutrals in a civil war is caused by wilful refusal to accept reason, which is surely contrary to your stated theme that the civil war was caused by an involuntary failure of communication between brothers. Exorcise that devil. Unless your book is so brief that you can treat only of your main theme, in which case they will readily adjust their expectations, readers will miss an aspect of civil wars with which they are familiar, that there can be no neutrals, and doubt the rounded truth of everything else you say because you tried too hard to prove your point and so became one-sided, a special-pleader, in the reader's mind not much better than a propagandist, in short, a liar.

Plot The plot describes a series of *events*, actions your characters take, and whatever happens to them, which will illustrate the themes you have listed – or that is the way we shall approach it in this book in order to achieve a clear view of what you intend. In truth, as we have seen, the whole thing, concept, themes, plot, characters, events, comes to the beginning author as a creative package deal, and even the old hand, building a publishable idea from scratch, will see large pieces whole, and other pieces out of sequence. Do not be afraid, when we start on the detailed planning of your novel in the next chapter, to jump forwards and backwards between the sheets on which you have written events and those on which you have written characters. The actual planning of a novel is in real life a lot messier than in this clinical description, for the experienced writer no less than for you.

Characters If you know the names of your characters, by all means write their names on a separate sheet of paper even at this stage.

AN EXTREMELY LIMITED WARRANTY

The methods applicable to the detailed planning of your book, starting in the next chapter, are designed to overcome two difficulties, common to all writing methods, with the least unproductive effort. It is worth describing these difficulties briefly so that you are not startled when you run into them.

The Jute Effect We really cannot discuss with straight faces 'the dichotomous nonconsanguinuity of constructive method and productive result' so, until someone else comes up with a short name or immodestly sticks his own monicker on it, let's call our first problem the Jute Effect. What happens is that the writer becomes discouraged by the large gap revealed between his pristine vision and the necessary planning procedure with its multiple compromises, and further confused because the planning method seems entirely tangential to the desired finished book. For instance, if character is so important, why is the next chapter about plot; why don't we start with character and stick to it? Why, a student put it, do we plan in a spiral if we intend writing in a straight line? The answer is that we plan in a spiral to straighten all the curves that would remain in the way of writing in a straight line if we didn't plan that way, but I can't prove it until you've done it. Those of you who have started to write a book without any method are now in a better position to understand than those who have not that the pitfalls and difficulties we are overcoming are essential learning experiences on the way to becoming a writer. Keep this firmly in mind: the procedure is designed to break the whole book into pieces that you can build up day by day without going wrong too often or too far and perhaps wrecking your book irrecoverably.

The accursed fecundity of your mind A writer appointed my mentor by a film company resented the casual way his student threw out ideas ('That bloody Jute thinks he's still a wunderkind of advertising' was reported as the kindest of his strictures) and wrote in a letter about a novel of mine that 'the accursed fecundity of your mind will forever prevent [your] being published'. The irony is that this fellow had an even wilder imagination. His problem was that he cowered before it instead of taming it. A garden is a wilderness on which someone has imposed a modicum of order. It is the rare professional who can handle his book whole and no one would bet money on even the most

76

talented novice to succeed – indeed, it is the most inventive who most need disciplined planning if they are not to become irretrievably bogged in the mazes of their minds. Most writers have no alternative to planning their books. Once you accept that you cannot swallow it whole, you're halfway there. The other half is to decide in advance that you will not panic when, either in the planning or the writing, the complexity of the unravelling strands appear way beyond your present skills. These are your own ideas, and your mind, a wonderfully fair judge, would not have them if you did not also possess the skill to handle them. The trick is to isolate a piece no bigger than you can handle in a single workshift and to tackle it with all your concentration and without worrying too much about its effect elsewhere. A book in the writing is like a puzzle, and similarly rewards only those who persevere.

5
PLOTTER'S CIRCLE:
CONSTRUCTING A DETAILED
OUTLINE

THE plot is the structure within which your characters will relate to your readers. On that ground alone it is worth close attention, because *anything* that touches your characters is important. Competence in plotting is also the minimum skill required from a writer and, at some levels in a few genres (mystery and crime, sci-fi and fantasy), you might still find publication even if imaginative plotting is the limit of your skill. A competent plot is a signal to an editor that you have a professional attitude and might develop.

The finest plot is, technically, nothing more than a series of things your characters do or that happen to them. It is an absurdly easy thing to construct once you have broken it into its proper component parts. Problems are caused by the pure size of the task creating confusion rather than by any intrinsic difficulty exceeding the mental grasp of any author. The right attitude is brisk and businesslike. Plotting is a menial task you have to do, like washing dishes or adding up chequebook stubs, before you can proceed to more pleasant and creative tasks like cooking food or expense accounts. Don't let anyone feed you mystical or academic bull about plot – it's a simple Taiwanese mechanical, a lazy susan turning around to serve up the day's writing assignment on the right day when you are ready to write it.

THE JOHN BRAINE MEMORIAL METHOD

Remember the caveat that you should read and grasp this book whole before starting to follow it step by step; it is doubly important for this section, which could otherwise trap you in the large complexities we discussed in the previous chapter. This is my variant of a method many writers have worked out for themselves by trial and error. Ernest Hemingway and John Braine did it before we were born; Mr Braine describes his version of the method in great detail in his book *Writing a Novel*, a book you should in any event have within reach because Braine is sound on many of the more metaphysical interactions of the writer and his work (especially if he is a novelist or biographer) that cannot find space in this book. The Method, despite its shortcomings, earns its place here because of its universality, because it is a stage passed through by all but a minority of writers, and the one and only tried and trusted method of a surprising number of professional writers.

The first draft Forget all the stuff about concepts, themes, events, plot and characters. Either make an outline of your story not exceeding five hundred words – that is, two double-spaced typewritten pages – or just sit down and write the first draft, starting at the beginning and working your way steadily towards the end, writing a set number of hours each day, seven days a week without exception, and not going back to rewrite or polish. If you need to know something presently outside your ken, make a note in the margin to find it out later. If you need to invent something, make a note in the margin to invent it later. The main thing is to write at white-hot speed so that you can finish this first draft while your enthusiasm lasts. Don't worry about characters: they will 'reveal themselves in their actions' (John Braine). Don't sweat any small stuff, or for that matter large stuff. Just get it all down. Let it all hang out. Tell the story from the beginning to the end; we'll worry about the structure later. Aim for 80,000 words but don't worry even if you see the novel will be short or, more often, over the length, or if you feel you are going off the rails. Just continue writing to the end. These things, and everything else that can go wrong except not finishing the first draft, do not matter because in this method the first draft is always scrapped and a new one written from scratch. That is not madness: this pre-disposable draft is proper preparation, like spending time cleaning dirt or old paint off a door you want to paint because if you don't the new paint won't adhere and you will have to start again.

Your first draft will probably take anything from six weeks to six months to complete, depending on how fast you write. Mr Braine's advice works out to about 175 words per hour for two hours a day; that would mean almost a year before you can see the first fruits of your labour. I consider that dangerously extended, but if you have a job and busy weekends that may be all you can manage. The sooner you can finish this first draft, the better. Chapter 9 contains general advice on desirable routines for the writer which may help you make your writing time as productive as possible.

The second stage When you reach the end of this draft, read it through if you like and then take a week to savour the feeling of achievement. Meanwhile put the typescript away; don't reread. After a week or longer, read it again. This time a great many shortcomings will strike you. Don't despair. Most professional writers' first efforts were equally wretched and were turned into publishable books by nothing more than a calm head and methodical work. Don't start patching up. This draft is intended to be scrapped. Its purpose is to reveal the characters to you so that you feel at home with them and can explain them better to readers of your *second* draft.

Now put this draft in a bottom drawer and lock it. Better advice is to burn this draft but apparently aspirant writers feel that is like throwing the baby out with the bathwater. You have no need to refer back to it: a week after you finished writing it every word should be firmly impressed on your mind. Nor need you feel particularly sentimental about it – it is discarded sandpaper from preparing a paint job.

The next step is the most important of your writing career. You must write a summary of your discarded draft to serve as an outline for your intended book. It should be no more than 2000 words of properly structured, grammatical sentences rather than notes. Its purpose is to describe a clear chain of motivation for whatever your characters do in the book. This summary justifies the flow of events from the viewpoint of your characters. Give these 2000 words six tries or a fortnight of your time. Stop when an 'organic unity' (John Braine again) of motivation and event is discernible, that is, when everything your characters do is done for a reason and the whole contains nothing that is not done for a reason.

Next, make a list of your characters' names, ages, peculiarities of appearance or dress, profession, education, etc. Just jot down the bare physical essentials as an aide memoire to keep beside you and refer to as you write. Characters will reveal themselves by their actions in your book and any big 'character description' outside the book is a waste of time. Now perform the necessary checks for libel, as already described on pages 52–4.

Break the storyline into a series of events. Since you have a sequentially motivated summary, the order of your events should be clear, as well as their number and the magnitude of each in relation to the whole. Each event should be time-specific. You should know the time something happens, morning or afternoon, day of the week, summer or winter. John Braine advises that as a matter of literary principle the action in a novel should cover no more than a year of real time and I agree though for the different practical reason that it causes the novice avoidable problems when he tries to cram more than a year of events into 80,000 words; when you are more skilled and perhaps writing longer books, you can forget this suggestion.

Do the bits of research you have noted as necessary. Get maps of all the real places your characters inhabit, or draw maps of those you invented but don't waste time on superfluous detail. The maps will prevent a possible break in your concentration when you suddenly discover that you don't know the relationship of some geographical feature to another.

Tone of voice Finally, before you sit down to write the second draft, you should discover the 'tone of voice' (Norman Podhoretz, *Making It*) of your book. The tone of voice can be determined most easily if you think of your characters in conversation with the reader. How will your character address the reader? What impression is the character trying to leave on the reader? Despite appearances, this is easier for the novelist than for those practising other branches of creative writing, because the novelist creates his characters in the light of the tone of voice he decides upon, and easiest of all for the first-time novelist, whose tone of voice most often comes to him as part of his original conception of the novel. However, even novelists should pay conscious attention to the tone of voice because getting it wrong also means getting the characters wrong – and the whole book goes wrong from that moment. Whereas most other kinds of mistake can be fixed in the rewriting or by scrapping only part of the manuscript, starting with the wrong tone of voice normally means starting all over again with a fresh draft.

Prose writers other than novelists have the problem of first perceiving the tone of voice of their characters and then conveying it faithfully. Again, it is worth much effort to get this right the first time. Recently I read all the available biographies of Eisenhower, who can be thumbnailed as a man who got things done. The hostile biographies leave one believing that Eisenhower was a sly hypocrite, a shirker and do-nothing, an idler and a buckpasser; the bad biographies even when favourable are not far off this mark. It may just be that the writers of the biographies which fail to catch Eisenhower's own tone grew up in cities as sophisticated competitors in rat races from a very early age, but certainly the authors of the best biographies either had the experience of growing up in a mickey mouse place such as Abilene was at the turn of the century or took the (admittedly very great) trouble to inform themselves of the ethos which shaped Eisenhower's life. Eisenhower was formed against a background where excellence was expected but braggadocio punished; where hard competition was the norm but a boy was required to show the modesty of waiting until leadership was urged upon him rather than claiming it as his right; where it was proper and Christian to give some of the credit due to you to less talented members of the team while accepting blame for their mistakes. In a harsh New York or prissy New England tone of voice, Eisenhower falls down dead; in a midwestern small town tone of voice this great internationalist speaks to us. You can see how easily the tone of voice influences the interpretation of the facts. Choosing the right tone of voice also allows his successful biographers to evaluate Eisenhower's achievements properly, whether favourably or unfavourably matters not (a good biography is never neutral), because it offers them insights into their subject's motivation not available to the rest.

A useful exercise is to try to spot the effect of choosing the wrong tone of voice in other people's books. Anthologies of travel pieces are especially illuminating because the best writers allow you to imagine yourself a Tuareg desert ranger or whatever; the writers who never let you forget that they, and you, are from a different culture are the ones who didn't catch the tone of voice of the people of Farawayandutterlyweird. Tone of voice, in the ultimate analysis, is the author getting inside his character. All else is surface.

Writing your second draft You should not allocate more than a day or two for discovering the tone of voice. If you do not have it by then, start writing. Since the right tone of voice is often inherent in the material, as in the Eisenhower example above and always in fiction, you may be able to express it in your prose without necessarily being able to articulate it as an abstract. If you have chosen the wrong tone of voice, that too will soon become apparent. Don't stop, junk what you have written and start again, hoping for something better. That is fatal. Carry on writing until you complete a section in the correct tone of voice, then start again from the beginning in that tone of voice, or carry on to the end of the book and then rewrite the first, bad part from scratch.

The second draft you can write quite slowly, testing each word and phrase on your tongue, as long as you write a set number of words or hours each day without fail. Or you can write it at the same white-hot speed you wrote the first draft. Either way you will have to polish it, as described in Chapter 7. However, because this is a completely new second draft, you will have to do less polishing than writers who follow other methods described below, so keep in mind that you are now writing for publication and posterity, not for your bottom drawer. Towards the end there will be a temptation to speed up to be done with a job at which you might by now have spent eighteen months. Resist it. Slow yourself consciously to be certain of doing your very best work because the end of your book is what remains most firmly in the reader's mind.

Pros and cons of The Method The huge advantage of the John Braine Memorial Method is that the novice and the professional alike can immediately satisfy that urge, which drives all real writers, to *write* his book, without the tedious technicalities of planning intervening. The second great advantage is that it fosters the right attitude by presupposing that your work is malleable, to the extent that you will write a complete draft just to throw away so that you can write a better one. Thirdly, if done properly, it can reduce the painful task of cutting, which Faulkner called 'murdering your darlings', to almost nothing, and the tedious but necessary business of rewriting and polishing to a minimum. The scale of these reductions may be clearer to the novice if he would consider that the burden of effort in all other methods of creating a book, in none of which the first draft is discarded in full, falls not so much on writing the first draft as cutting and rewriting parts of it in a continuous cycle until the whole thing is in any event rewritten.

Then why does not everyone follow The Method? Wherefore the rest of this chapter? The problem with The Method is that the disadvantages match the scale of the advantages.

First, and most important even for the professional writer who assumes, often incorrectly, that his experience will prevent things going wrong, The Method consumes much more time than the other methods even when everything goes right; this might be important to a novice as well, especially if he has another job which limits his writing time. Second, things might go wrong. The main reason many new writers give up after the first draft is that they cannot find a way of unifying a huge florid structure into a persuasive chain of motivation. Or the second draft might, even in professional hands, need quite as much cutting, rewriting and polishing as that created by other methods, in which case the time spent on the first, disposable and disposed, draft is wasted. Third, The Method is inflexible: you cannot switch out of it to other methods, which all assume some degree of *pre-planning*, when halfway through you discover you don't like it or it doesn't work for you. The Method, to be blunt, permanently loses us the talents of some would-be writers who with other methods might not have given up and taken up power-boating instead. Fourth, The Method, because in the main it deals with the book whole, is loaded with the difficulties attendant on transmitting such a large creative concept to paper over an extended period of time. These are collectively known as writer's blocks but, as we will see in the appropriate place, are for the most part nothing more than a lack of proper preparation – but of a kind for which The Method makes only scant provision.

The Method stands by itself. The alternative methods that follow are all complementary, a mix-and-match grab-bag from which you choose only what is congenial to you and discard whatever job lot does not suit you.

THE CORRECT FRAME OF MIND

In weighing techniques for controlling and channelling imaginative insights into a large-scale long-term project, remember always their purpose, which is nothing more fanciful than to cut your dream into bite-sized pieces so that the size of your conception doesn't stop you dead, perhaps for good. What is a bite-size? For the novice it should probably be a maximum of one day or a minimum of one workshift. Until experience teaches you otherwise, which will happen very quickly, you should consider as bite-sized the amount of work you can reasonably do in two hours; in Chapter 9 there is a discussion of concentration spans and other factors affecting your work methods and routines.

Concept and theme via event into plot You have your concept, which is defined as the vision of the whole book you already carry in your head and wish to leave your reader with; you have written it down in a single brief sentence without qualifying clauses. Put it aside now until you have finished the book, when you might ask, Have I achieved my vision? You also have a handful of themes, some of them perhaps with sub-themes, which together build your concept. All of these should fit on a single sheet of paper. They are abstracts and will come to life only when peopled with characters. But characters do not live in a vacuum. They do things. Things happen to them. The plot is the structure within which these 'things' happen. We shall call the 'things that happen' *events*. A group of events together illustrate a theme. A plot is an assembled group of events: it is assembled for logic and order according to some narrative standard which is defined by your concept and themes and by literary convention.

Note that every narrative, which includes all creative literature such as biography or memoirs or travel or history, has a plot even if it is only the most rudimentary beginning-middle-end of the dullest life or journey. Note too that there is no writing without characters. Even how-to books have characters – in this book you and I are the main characters, with as subsidiary characters a bunch of writers whom I know either personally or through their work, plus a few cameos by students or non-writing friends who have particularly striking experiences to relate.

86

To summarise: We want a framework within which your characters can act and develop in a structured manner so that the events of which they partake will illuminate the themes of your work so that the concept can be perceived whole and unblemished by the reader.

Events Suppose we are writing a book – it could be a novel, a biographical fraction or faction, or history of subrosa diplomacy – about the secret mission of Sir Basil Zaharoff to Germany in 1918 which some believe stopped the war a year earlier than would otherwise have been possible. Here are some events: 'Z receives mission from Lloyd George and Clemenceau'; 'Z briefs Nadel'; 'Z and Nadel acquire identity papers – how precisely? refer McCormick'; 'Arrangements are made for doubles'; 'Z and Nadel pose as revolutionaries in Zurich'.

The event is written down as briefly as possible. If, in the moment of writing it down, you discover that you don't know some relevant fact you will have to discover or invent, make a note of it, as in the note about referring a query to Donald McCormick, the world's leading authority on Zaharoff and his only reliable biographer. Note that the events are not necessarily in order. You can worry about order later; for the moment, just write down every major event you can think of. Premature attempts at chronology can be very destructive, so put it off as long as possible.

If you now discover that your splendid vision is rather sparsely populated with the hard tack that actually makes a book, don't panic. It happens to the best of us. Refer to your themes if you begin to run out of breath, because they are certain to suggest events that would be essential for their illustration. Refer to your list of characters, because considering their names and real or imagined characteristics is certain to suggest something they will say or do (or, in the case of historical or other real-life characters, have said or done) that will put in train something else, a consequence, in short, an event. Just before despair overtakes you, read the list of events you have already written down: some of them will be rather large chunks which must obviously be broken down, and in doing so will suggest something else. 'The Burning of Atlanta' didn't happen all at once. Or, to stick to our Zaharoff example: the mission isn't just handed over like a bill dropping through the letterbox. 'Arrival of statesmen – other pols in anteroom'; 'LlG and C describe situation and mission over 36-place gold setting while Z prepares salad at table'; 'Doubts and cynicism of LlG and C in their car afterwards'; 'Arrangements to second Nadel from Surete to Z'; 'Z considers N's history – Mouchlou naturalisation episode'.

How many events? This is a how-long-is-a-piece-of-string question. The answer is: The minimum to do the job right. Remember, no publisher prints the perfect plot; he prints the resulting book. (And this kind of plotting has very little to do with writing proposals you can sell to publishers before you have actually written the book, or with creating a representative and persuasive synopsis of a book you have written. Those are different skills, applied to different purposes, approached differently. You do not need to learn them until you are established.) For each of your themes you need only the minimum of events to illustrate that theme completely. Even in an all-action adventure, you are hardly likely to require or be able to fit an average of more than one event to every two pages – properly planned comics, which must be the tightest possible format to work in, try to have a major event on every double-page spread. Two pages (double-spaced typewriter measure, say around 500 words) is also the minimum you should try to write in your two-hour workshift, until experience teaches you better.

Effectively, this means that, if your planned book is to be 300 pages long, your plot notes should not exceed about 150 events. Since each event-note, if it is longer than a mere note, should not be longer than two or three lines, we are talking of an absolute maximum of six or seven single-spaced pages of events. This is not an attempt to mechanise a creative act but to protect you from the natural temptation to dawdle over easy inconsequentials.

In real life, the events in a plot outline are that many only in two instances. The first is the novice author who is covering all bets or, more likely, expanding the preliminary work to fill the time because he naturally fears the unknown next step of dealing with characters. The second is a very special though not rare case found most often in television series-serial (soap) production: the outline for a screenplay in master scene synopses where every master scene will be numbered and will contain a description of the event(s), sometimes with a timing in seconds that the scene should occupy, *outside of which no or very little invention is allowed* to the writer assigned to the script because that will interfere with storylines in future episodes which may already be assigned, written, or even in the can.

Don't sweat it Overdoing plotting is self-destructive. Writers of tele-soaps don't burn out through self-disgust at working in a trash medium for megabucks – that's a myth fostered by fellows who failed to make the grade – but because such precision work creates stress and tension. It's writing by numbers, and marking up the numbers yourself makes no difference. Professional writers know, right from the planning stage, to allow themselves lots of leeway for discovering in the actual writing the felicities of plot and character which raise the small chuckles of satisfaction that make long lonely days in front of a white wall bearable. The creative act needs breathing room.

A normally phlegmatic editor surprised me in a discussion of plotting: his beef was neither incompetent plotting, nor over-plotting (in the sense of too much plot), but the deleterious effect of effort misspent on plotting on the writing of otherwise promising novices.

With experience your need for detailed plotting will decrease. My own books are thought by students of these things to be very heavily plotted. But their event-sheets numbered three pages in the beginning and have now been reduced to one which is hardly ever full.

Don't give more than a day to writing down events. Others will come to you when you sort them or when you start working with characters. It is better to have too few than too many. They are not ends in themselves so it doesn't matter when you attend to them. On the second day, start working the events you have into your plot.

STRUCTURE AS A CREATIVE TOOL

The majority of literary formats recognised in classrooms are academic mirages, useful either for analysing the work of dead writers who can't complain or, like Post-Structuralism, for presenting literature as the handmaiden of some crazed political creed, but utterly useless to the practising writer. The fellows in the hard sciences are right when they say that a theory, to be useful, must explain both the construction and deconstruction of any matter; by that test literature, and most creative writing, as taught today is paraplegic and should be pensioned off. But there are a few older theories, discarded by academia as too simple to impress anyone, which are of use to the writer seeking help in sorting his events.

Beginning, middle and end Man crawls before he can walk and walks before he runs. The same goes for a story. Certain of your events obviously must happen before others *can* happen. Sort your slips of paper or index cards containing events into that order. Not all will fit. Don't worry, one of the other methods will slot them in. But the beginning, middle and end should take care of the most obvious events. It is also useful to return to as a test: when you have sorted all your events, does the order not suggest gaps, events that should be in your story to complete the motivation of some theme but are missing?

A small problem, easily overcome There is no harm in sorting your pieces of paper by theme, for the time being anyway, to reassure yourself that you have enough to illustrate all themes. But don't number them in that order or do anything else that will fix them in your mind in that order. It is rare for themes to have a natural chronology even in the crudest non-fiction, and unheard-of in fiction.

Themes are separated in our planning merely for convenience and intertwine in the story – by having their events mixed up for other narrative purposes, mainly tension – to be blended only at the end, when you leave the reader with your whole concept. Don't sweat it: you have already proved, by conceiving a book whole, that you can handle large, complicated mental structures.

A mountain of climaxes It is axiomatic that near the end of your book there will be a major climax. Even historians and serious biographers, who if they are honest frequently cannot choose the climax of their story as the place to stop writing, often put the after-effects they perforce must describe into a chapter labelled 'Epilogue', a clever way of signalling to the reader that the exciting action is past and what comes now is decline and obscurity. Put the event that describes the final climax at the back. Now consider the rest.

Any book but the shortest is like a major mountain. You don't climb steadily to a peak. You climb a foothill, reach a peak, walk downhill for another while, climb a less gentle slope to a higher peak, walk down into the next valley before ascending a steeper hill to a still higher peak. Near the very top of the mountain the climb is likely to be almost perpendicular. The peaks are climaxes in the story, the steepness of the ascent the pace of the story which at this stage in the planning is represented by the spacing and expected length (when fully written) of events. Do not spend time worrying about pace; one does not plan for pace, one writes for it, one cuts for it, one rewrites for it.

If you now choose your subsidiary climaxes and slot them into their places, you can often see immediately which of the remaining events should lead up to which climax and even in which order. And, again, you can see which climactic events need an establishing lead-in of events that will now suggest themselves to fill the gap.

Two traps This climaxes method is tricky, not intrinsically but for those who have a formal literary education or are widely read in the more pretentious of modern writings on literature. Such sophisticates bring to the craft of writing an entirely unwarranted assumption that the climax-series is necessarily progressive or even geometric. It is not. If you try to create each and every climax greater than the last – not even to mention the foolishness of trying to create it greater by a formula amount – you lock your book into a posture your characters will probably reject, something that will be obvious to your editor and your reader. This anthropomorphism ('characters will reject') is indulged to emphasise that the plot is only a notional framework to be inhabited by characters whose lives and reactions do not proceed by mathematical formulae. It doesn't even work in fiction. If some of your peaks are lower than the preceding peaks, and even if your final peak is not truly the highest in the book, so what? As long as the positioning is properly motivated by event and character, the reader will be much more inclined to view it as a reflection of skill on your part in handling real characters and situations than as a mistake.

Sometimes one hears talk of a 'climax-anticlimax cycle', which is a classic example of the nonsense put out by academics never likely to write anything real people might read voluntarily; it is significant that their examples are, and can be, drawn only from a few modern writers not read by anyone off-campus. An anticlimax is a narrative development that bears no fruit or has an opposite outcome to that which reason and literary convention would lead one to expect. Professional writers believe in red herrings, not in swindling readers with disclaimers of their duty of imagination.

Endings It is highly likely that the ending is the part of your book most highly developed in your mind, possibly already set in a near-final form. You know instinctively that 'the end informs the beginning' (Iris Murdoch). Experienced writers often cut down on the amount of work involved in planning by actually writing the closing pages (paragraphs, sections, chapters) and then planning the rest of the book towards that ending. Katherine Anne Porter goes as far as to state this as an act of faith: 'If I didn't know the ending of a story, I wouldn't begin. I always write my last line, my last paragraph, my last page first.'

Set pieces If you now apply this method to each of the smaller endings, your intervening climaxes, by writing them first, you will have a series of set pieces of the high spots in your novel. Think of set pieces as the battle scenes in a Shakespeare play and you will instantly understand that they can be small or large and of varying intensity and intention stretching right across the affective spectrum to farce and bathos. Your set pieces will be a similar mix. It then remains for you to write in each section towards the climax.

Unfortunately this method pools all the excitement at one end of the job and leaves you with a lot of the less exciting development work which will take several times as long to write. However, if you can live with this disadvantage, your noted events in their order may be all the detailed plotting you need.

Beginnings The new writer, who has carried the gravid germ of his book around in his mind for longer than he will ever carry a second or subsequent book, usually also has a good idea of the precise beginning he wants and could probably write a good few pages before he gets stuck. If this describes you, go for it, because the more you can put down without the intervention of essentially arid planning methods, the easier the material will be for you to write and, given proper rewriting in its place, for the reader to believe.

Openings have almost always to be rewritten in the light of changes from the conception you choose or are forced to make further on in the book. This applies to everyone, including professional writers, but even more to the novice, who is learning his trade as he writes the book and should finish it vastly better equipped – among other things to write a better opening – than when he started. But you should still make your first attempt at the opening the best you can, because what the characters do in it shapes the rest of the book.

93

I can do it, I can do it! A point will arrive when you will note a few key climaxes on a sheet of paper more as a security blanket than anything else and you can start writing a book at the beginning or anywhere else with perfect certainty of finishing it. But don't judge your professional progress by the amount of planning you have to do. Many professional writers still go the full planning hog with every book.

There are a few writers who expand these few notes we have been talking about, then expand them again, and so on until they have a book. This is most emphatically not a recommended procedure except to the timorous and strictly 'literary', because the output of this method seems (to me at least) to consist entirely of novels about writers writing novels, stiff considerations of trends in literature or history or whatever, in fact a harsh underlining of my warning that the planning method is dead, in the sense of Lawrence's table and snake analogy,* and should be separated from the writing if you desire the book to be quick. In this regard the electronic outliners available for use with microcomputers as stand-alone applications or integrated into wordprocessors are a curse, because they are designed for exactly that sort of expansion of lifeless notes into large lifeless documents; the best of them honestly calls itself a 'presentations processor', which tells you where it belongs.

A VISUAL CONSTRUCTION

A whole generation of writers and aspirants have now grown up with television as an established fact of life. Such writers are bound to have a more visual approach to writing than earlier writers, who inevitably took more of their experience of life from books than from film. Writers with a visual approach, and those trying to force spreading plots into confined spaces, might with profit use the plot outline in master-scene synopses as a planning tool for writing prose. It is a favourite of mine because it saves so much

*D. H. Lawrence, asked to define 'quick and dead', first pointed to a drinking snake, then rapped the table at which he sat.

cutting agony and rewriting time and frustration by pointing up, in concise format, the excesses that can be cut from the plot before writing commences, and the holes which have to be filled before the reader can grasp continuous motivated sense from the story.

A scene is the action between one camera cut and the next, and a master scene is all the action between first sight of any location and the cut to another location. A scene in film terms is too brief for our purposes but the master scene is almost equivalent to the event we have already defined, and where it is less, because an event unlike a master scene can take in more than one location, the event can be made up by grouping two or more master scenes. Here is the simple format:

51. **EXT/INT. FILTON, MISS. AFTERNOON &
EVENING.**
Describe town in specifics or in Marshall's reasoning, that is, generic mid-America? Churchill delivers his 'Iron Curtain' speech. Audience reaction muted horror – Marshall's point. Truman telegram. Caviare incident at dinner afterwards.

Notice that several locations – the town, the hall, the dean's house – are all covered under one heading for the convenience of the prose writer, whereas a real master scene synopsis for film would split this into at least three master scenes and quite probably ten (including establishing shots). But the prose writer will probably wish to handle the whole thing as one section, taking the content and effect of Churchill's speech as of a piece with the intentions of his ultimate hosts, Marshall and Truman, against the backdrop of the electorate they have to satisfy. Note also that not all the writer's decisions are yet made, but that all salient choices and already-chosen events, such as the caviare incident, are mentioned as aides memoire.

Number all master scenes in sequence. Each one has a heading telling you exactly where it is set and the time of day. The description of the event is brief, concise, merely a reminder of the high points.

And this is the way to describe a more complicated format with simultaneous events:

INTERCUT 51/52/53:
51. INT. WAREHOUSE. AFTERNOON
Paxton tortures Lydia for the code. The Arabs leer.

52. EXT. MOUNTAIN ROAD. AFTERNOON.
Bill races to save Lydia from a fate worse than death.

FLASHBACK IN LYDIA'S MIND:
53. EXT. RIVERBANK. MORNING.
Idyllic moment. Lydia in swing. Bill pushes her out over water; she screams in fright.

Try this method and, if you do not find it confining, as some do, use it either in preference to the other methods listed above or as a final tidying-up operation to give shape and form and order to your bits of paper containing events. If you have a word processor, the synopsis in master scenes as if for film is a quick plotter because you can go back and forth inserting events or moving them and have the electronics do the renumbering.

CHARACTER WITHIN PLOT

The whole of the next chapter is devoted to character creation and development but, as we have seen several times, the plot and the characters cannot and should not be separated, and in practice you will frequently move from your plotting sheets of paper to those on which your characters are listed and back again. However, even in the plotting stages of planning you should keep very firmly in mind that character is king.

The primacy of character Even before you write a word, you must check that the plot turns about the characters and not the other way round. Pay attention to the phrasing of events. Continuing with the *Zaharoff* example: 'Z considers Nadel's history' is personalised to the chief character. Three

96

or four books earlier I would probably have written 'Tell about Nadel's part in Mouchlou church burning'. That 'tell' is a dead giveaway. Description is a waste when instead you can communicate the same facts by showing your characters in action. This applies also to non-fiction. If you name your five most readable historians – of anything – and then consider what their writing style has in common, emphasis on the actions of the characters will feature prominently. The author telling the reader something isn't an event; it's in danger of becoming one of those boring bits most readers skip that Elmore Leonard says he leaves out of his books. By presenting the necessary background information in an action of one of the characters – the mental activity of considering the character of a companion in a dangerous task – it becomes an event readers want to know about. Work through your plot and rewrite every event as an action of a character major or minor, or seen from his viewpoint, or involving him somehow. Any 'event' that does not involve a character is description and therefore *ipso facto* not an event. About every event, ask Lenin's questions, 'Who does what to whom?', 'Who benefits?', 'Why?'

Character-generated plot One important reason for considering your plot the least of your creations and permanently malleable – open to the right offers – is that, in the writing, your characters will, if you have developed them right, surprise you. This is not anthropomorphism. Think of the most boring person you know. Has he never surprised you by doing something unexpected? We can never know anyone perfectly and creating a character in a book is a process of discovery for the author as much as for the reader. It should therefore be no surprise when a character under pressure of events seems to develop traits that you had not included in his original conception, or that these traits, especially in combination – friction – with those of the other characters, create new plot possibilities. If the newly possible events contribute towards illustrating your themes, by all means include them or substitute them for those that now seem pale by comparison.

97

TENSION

Tension makes your reader want to read on, to know what happens next. How it is achieved is a matter open to controversy but the metaphysics need not bother us more than passingly. We will concentrate on the technical means whereby a writer of goodwill can generate tension for the reader. We shall, however, take it as axiomatic that the reader demands tension: he does not want to be bored. Note that tension, though often loosely spoken of as if only a fictional device, is a factor in the relationship of the reader to every kind of narrative literature, even if only at the malicious next-trick-please level: '...but the question now is, can Mr Brownjims keep the dialectical ball in the air.'

Plot as potential tensional framework Whoever tells you the plot achieves tension has not thought the matter through. It is true that the events of the plot, in the correct order, have the potential for tension. But try telling the plot of your book to anyone without once referring to a person in the story ('He did this and then she did that'). Beside my chair lies an academic book on the history of imagination written by a man obviously more interested in theorising on abstract philosophy than in character, yet in his index the preponderance of names of people outweighs all the other entries together by a factor of over sixty to one. The plot is made flesh only in man. Your reader's connection with you, the writer, is not through the plot but through the character. The reader identifies with the character rather than the situation. It took several years of listening to would-be writers for me to grasp that many of them did not understand an obvious truth: you must present the character for identification before the reader will develop fellow-feeling for him. This is not a mechanical matter but one of the right outlook, of where you're starting from. If you devise a plot and people it with cardboard cut-outs going through the motions prescribed by the plot, you don't even get cardboard cut-out reactions from readers – you get nothing. Some really fabulous, wish-I'd-thought-of-it-first, thriller plots of the last ten years failed with readers because the potential tension remained unrealised in the absence of characters the readers could relate to. If that can happen to thrillers, supposedly all about plot... It is one of the few inflexible rules of lasting writing that readers care enough about the characters to want to know what they will do next. That's all tension is. It is everything: no literature without tension, no tension without credible characters.

Writing tension In practice you don't plan for tension, even in a thriller or adventure, because another literary convention – your series of more or less escalating climaxes, and the build-up to each – takes care of the overall mechanics of tension without much conscious thought. Tension is not a tool, but a result. You write or rewrite for tension, so that building tension becomes part of your style. Given that readers identify with your characters, there are however some mechanical tensioning devices you can and should build in for the extra edge of 'unputdownability' with publishers and readers.

Openings A publisher will usually read no more than ten pages of a novel he rejects and most often only the first page. A member of the public trying to decide whether your book is worth buying or borrowing from a library reads the dust jacket or paperback blurb and then, very probably, the first few lines of the opening chapter. On this he makes a decision. You don't sell to either publisher or reader unless you can grab and hold them right at the beginning. The implication for your opening sections is clear. All professionals rewrite extensively but the most rewritten part of any pro's book is probably the first chapter or section.

The first section of the aspirant's first book is comparatively in even greater need of recasting because not only was it written when the novice was at his rawest, but, as the part of his book he gestated longest and most lovingly, it is often the most precious. Precious, in any publishing office, is not a word meaning valuable; it is used scathingly to mean pretentious and affected. Rewrite it in the light of your improved skills and understanding of the characters.

Meanwhile back at the monkey-house The reader doesn't read letters and form words from them. He reads whole words six or seven at a time, phrases, lines, even sentences if they are not too long, all at a gulp. The technical term for the group of characters the eye takes in at one shot is 'a saccad' and the best print designers try to choose column-widths to suit the saccadic rhythm of the material because the saccad determines the most easily grasped line length. The concept of the saccad also has implications for the writer, including several important guidelines to building tension.

But start at the top. First, consider the totality of your book. Is there any reason except tradition for breaking it into chapters of roughly equal length? The traditional reason is that books were read aloud in instalments in country houses and had therefore to be cut to a length that could comfortably be read aloud in an evening. Except if you are a writer of books that are intended to be read aloud, for instance children's books, or that must give readers a break now and again, is there any reason for chapters at all?

The contents list of my novel *Iditarod* (illustrated right), about the eponymous race, is a rare example of a traditional form being in sympathy with a modern tale, the race in the story being perfectly matched to the countdown shape offered by the numbered chapters.

CONTENTS

Breaks that do not follow the natural flow of the story should have a purpose beyond blind tradition-mongering. Normally this purpose is to enhance tension, so that you place the break where the break itself communicates an expectation of heightened tension to the reader, or leaves him hanging for a breathless moment through that line-space if the heroine is already in dire jeopardy of a fate worse than death. Or you might break at the change of setting or mood. Many people who read *Sinkhole*, a disaster novel, talk to me in terms of every second counting for the characters, of what a novelist thinks of as telescoped time-frames. This is not a serendipitous impression: every section is headed with a clock-reading exact to the minute, precisely so that readers might know that time rather than the bravery of rescuers, which in real life as in fiction can be taken for granted, is the great constraint threatening the lives of the surviving victims. The technique is not new; I took it from Richard Martin Stern, who may or may not have originated it. Most writers never put a new format into circulation; all of us use uncountable formats and devices created by our predecessors. Just be certain that whatever device you use is apt to the circumstances of your material: the same timing trick would merely look cheap if applied to the rising and ablutions of some office worker climaxing in catching the bus to work. As of now, you should take mention of a 'section' as any part of your book defined between two breaks, even if those breaks are only line-spaces.

If possible, each section-ending should have a hook leading the reader into the next section. 'Thus, driven by Man and Nature, the wolfpack would intersect fatally with the dog-sled racers.' This is the last line from one of the two-page sections of the parallel story of the wolves in *Iditarod*. It will be several big sections yet before the wolves and the racers actually intersect, but it summarises what has gone immediately before, and the next section, already visible to the reader, *who cannot stop himself reading the first saccad*, deals with the racers. No matter how late the hour, he wants to read on to discover which of the racers the wolfpack will eat or how many wolves the racers will kill, depending on whose side he has taken.

It is a good idea to have both a sharp hook in the last line of any section and a sparkling start in the opening line of the next, but of the two the most important is the start of the next section. The brilliant journalist and public relations expert Theo Martins once wrote down the notorious never-ending joke of the man who found the lost dog and claimed the reward. His opening line was, 'Not that shaggy, sir.' He explained that after intriguing your readers with the thought *Why should the writer give away his punchline?* you had them hooked to the end of the story, trying to answer their own question. It was the only way of keeping them reading a story everyone already knew. Of course you need not give away your punchline, but the best starts certainly raise questions for readers. Who? What? Why? When? Where? How? Who? Who? Who? Here are some starter lines, with explanations where required, taken at random from Andrew McCoy's *Small War, Far Away*, which tells of Lance Weber and his family and friends on the run from the Argentinian Army during the Falklands war:

'Lance Weber, fighting for his life, had no time to...' The first line in the book. What follows immediately is a description of systems of justice in ex-colonies of ex-Great Powers, plus a digression on architecture, but the reader wants to know why Weber is fighting for his life in these elegant surroundings and reads on.

'Over breakfast, which they had at a table set in the orange grove beyond the moat...' Wouldn't you like to know more about people who live like this?

'Lance looked down at the water below his feet and said into the mike attached to his crash helmet...' This is the first line after a major part-title which signifies the passage of several years, and enters straight into action without explanation; the reader must read on to find out why Lance is swaying in a harness slung from a helicopter.

'Ruby knew something was badly wrong when...'

'Something was coming to Hernandez but not what he had expected nor from a direction he was looking to.'

What? From whom? Would it be justice at last?

'Jerez was desperate.' And what would he do about it?

'At dawn on their third day in the hide...'

'The soldiers came on the fourth day.' And did they discover our fugitives?

'The air attaché cursed the French political system.' Why? What does it have to do with our story? (It had better, or the reader will lose interest.) Note that there is tension here between the reader and the author as well as between the reader and the characters he roots for, who have been temporarily shoved offstage by this apparent irrelevance.

'Hernandez, stomach sour, buttocks clenching...'

'They stood transfixed upon...'

'Places you can hide four large vehicles and ten people...'

'It was a journey that would haunt their nightmares...'

'But it was not a fragmentation grenade.' We had left the hero for dead many pages before, with a nastily precise description of what fragmentation grenades can do. The interlude was gripping enough. Now we're back with the hero, and the fragmentation grenade links the two episodes in the reader's mind.

'Hernandez heard about the flares four hours later.'

'Hernandez fumed and threatened but...'

'Lance watched the radar most unhappily.' The reader already knows that when this quintessential hard man becomes unhappy, a baddy gets what's coming to him. Since there are obviously very few pages left in the book when we read this line, it creates a lip-smacking anticipation that Hernandez and Jerez will at last get what they have deserved many times over.

You could choose similar section-opening lines from almost any professional writer's book, regardless of his subject or genre. The lines in themselves are not show-stoppers and will win no prizes in literary competitions. Their intention is the very opposite: to ease the reader unobtrusively but inexorably over the dangerous lull where he might conceivably put the book down, never to pick it up again, and into the next section. To stop the reader with pyrotechnic writing would defeat the purpose; save that for a few lines hence, when you have the reader in the palm of your hand – at least until the next section break.

The ending Your story ends when all your themes are fully explicated so that your concept is born in the reader's mind to stick there like a burr, causing him never to forget your name, right? No, wrong. Your story must end on, or not too far beyond, a major climax. That is a convention readers are happy with and only amateurs disappoint readers' expectations for the sake of burnishing their own egos by a display of contempt for their paymasters. It needn't be the biggest climax in the book but it must be a solid one. That is the first important constraint on the perfect book.

The second constraint on the perfect book is the perception of perfection itself. Readers are people, and observe other people every day of their lives: they know perfection of character is a mirage. If you agree that a book in any of our fields is primarily about character, then it follows that the perfectly plotted and written book will be so unreal as to be bland, perhaps even chilling, because it will lack those slightly rough edges of real-world characters. Elsewhere I wrote that you must plot in an Agatha Christie frame of mind but write with human frailty to the forefront; this has earned me a lot of grief from the kind of person who can list the inconsistencies in all Agatha Christie's books, which turn out, on investigation, all to be caused by the characters rather than deficiencies in their creator's plotting – she was a lot smarter than many of her critics.

By all means write the extra scenes that will explicate your themes to their fullest. In the rewriting you might be able to move them to an earlier part of the narrative where they could add to the tension. But try to prepare yourself mentally to do without them. Readers are intelligent people: they do not need every i dotted and every t crossed. Their minds, given a bare sufficiency of information and clues, will make the perceptive closure to the whole. No professional writer thinks that too much plot is better than too little.

DEVELOPMENT AND CONTROL

The plot, written down, broken into events in sequential order, is not, repeat not, graven on stone. In practice you will find that all kinds of interesting highways and byways open up in the writing. What to do? There are writers who follow the worked-out plot religiously without the smallest deviation and a smaller number who invariably try all exciting possibilities. The argument for going where the characters carry the plot is that, given that the characters are properly defined and developed, forcing them into the confines of the set plot stultifies their development and therefore denies the narrative a large measure of the reader-identification that comes from fully developed characters; in the worst case, close adherence to the plot can destroy the characters and with them the book itself. The argument against detouring from a properly developed plot is that, in a distressing number of cases, especially among novices, the divergence from the plot is nothing but an authorial indulgence – which is guaranteed to damage the book. The underpinning rationale most often offered by adherents to the worked-out plot is that any kind of narrative creative writing is a *composition* and that those who want to diverge from the structural implications of composed writing should write in the established form for wandering minds making odd connections – the essay. If you feel inspiration coming on, says this school, lie down until it passes. This is generally sound advice, with only two exceptions: the large insight into a whole concept that will become a book, and the insight which illuminates a character and sends him off in new directions.

Neither argument is overwhelming because adherence to one or the other is too obviously determined by a writer's personality. You will have to decide for yourself what you do if the choice of following the plot you have slaved over conflicts with a distinctly different direction indicated by your characters. If you do diverge, make a note of precisely where you parted from the worked-out plot – and where you returned to it – so that later you can weigh whatever you wrote 'under instant inspiration' critically during the cutting and rewriting process.

For the writer of history or biography this problem is rarer, but especially acute when it arises because the historical facts of the 'plot' have of course still to be honoured. Three questions will have to be asked and answered. Is your problem caused by a misconception about the character you are writing about and his motivations, that is, have you understood him sufficiently? Think back to our Eisenhower example (pages 82–3), where those biographers who did not see the barefoot boy behind the conqueror failed to understand anything else. Are you attempting to force a prejudgement on the actions of your characters which bears no relation to reality, and that is perhaps politically or morally inspired? If you have to bend the character to fit an interpretation of results, you're in trouble and must think again or resign yourself to being read and believed only by those who already share your prejudices. Have you selected the most important themes illustrated by your character's actions or are you dealing with what he himself would have considered a minor byproduct or had not foreseen at all as a consequence of his actions? This variant of the failure to understand a character gets a particularised entry of its own in our list of questions because it is so common, and responsible for so much of the petty and pettyfogging hatchetwork in history and biography written by people with twenty-twenty hindsight who never in their lives had to take a critical decision under mortal pressure, and who refuse to understand that morality is not a fixed quantity in every generation.

If your mind threatens to go into thermal overload with all the complications of plotting, take heart. The message of the next chapter is that, in every kind of narrative writing, character is everything. And character in its literary sense, as you will grasp after only a little application, is very easy to understand. Once you understand character, whole books drop into place, cutting and rewriting become almost a pleasure, and tiresome blocks and complexities disappear as if they never existed.

6
QUICK OR DEAD
CREATING LIVING
CHARACTERS

E VERY narrative stands or falls by its characters. That is axiomatic. If you do not believe that, no-one can help you become a published writer. Belief in character is the second impetus towards becoming a writer. Perseverance will get you published; command of character will make you a good writer. Reprise:

Character is the link between your reader and your book's 'plot', the glue that sticks them together inseparably.

Character is the link between your reader and you, the writer. If the reader does not believe in your characters, he will not believe in your authority as a writer.

Character is the catalyst of tension. If the reader does not care enough about the character to want to know what happens to him, there is no tension. No tension, no story. No story, no publication.

Character is the ultimate plot-creator. People doing things *for a reason* and the consequences of their actions – what we have labelled events – make up a story.

Character, as a consequence, is gold in every commercial publisher's boardroom and ditto in the offices of every competent semi-commercial and specialist press likely to be interested in narrative prose of any kind. This by itself is a good reason to pay attention: a few publishers driven by greed or fear can behave like philistines but the industry consensus is usually wise and on character it is unanimous. It is easy to point to books with cardboard cut-outs promoted to bestsellerdom but there is always a reason (very often that the author's earlier well-characterised book was a best-seller), and virtually all books by first authors to which publishers give big promotion have fully realised characters. Get your characters right and publishers will forgive you anything – and rightly so. Good characterisation is the highest form of narrative art and publishers, like writers, know it.

Character is the tool the writer uses to solve all the problems we have met in the preceding chapters and most of those in the chapters to follow.

Unfortunately, good characterisation is also by far the most difficult of the skills an author has to learn. That is not to say it is impossible, or even as difficult as solving simultaneous equations in algebra. A motivational expert, who makes a fine living training high-level international salesmen, listened to me for a couple of hours on characterisation before exclaiming, 'But that's precisely what I tell my boys: Personalise everything! Live through your customer!' Substitute 'character' for customer – and now tell me you can't learn to do anything a salesman lusting for promotion can.

Once you wholeheartedly accept the primacy of character as an act of almost religious faith, the rest comes with practice at the detail-work of your characters; it is a matter of perseverance at discovering and developing skills you already have rather than of innate talent. Hold on tight to that thought when the going gets tough.

It is also useful to consider everything else the writer does as the more or less mechanical, if essential, support structure to the creative act of characterisation, so that whatever you do, be it splitting events into bite-sizes or ordering them into a plot, or writing or rewriting your book, or creating the most tense of action scenes, one eye is always kept firmly on your characters.

Character is the core of our craft. It follows that this chapter must be the core of this book. However, don't sweat it as you would a theoretical text. This chapter should in the first instance benefit you in two specific ways: it should leave you with a firm belief in the primacy of character; and it should act as a base on which you can develop your own character-building methods (which will contribute very largely to your unique style). You will therefore learn to understand and use what is in it, and how it relates to the references to character liberally scattered in the other chapters, a lot more easily and also more productively if you start writing your own book immediately after reading to the end of this book.

CREATING CHARACTERS

It is a pleasing conceit of authors to say that they create their characters consciously, because that gives the impression they know what they are about: professional, purposeful men and women in the march of progress.

Sources of characters Generally speaking, however, the writer's major conscious effort is expended not in the creation of the character but in drawing him forth from the recesses of the subconscious where he has lain dormant, perhaps for years, and then stepping back at the right moment so that the character can have breathing-space to develop in the writing, apparently independently of its roots. Professional writers do not like admitting to this process because it makes them look like idiots not quite in control of their destiny, and because characters admitted to be drawn from the subconscious make an ideal recipe for libel suits brought by litigants who do not understand how the mind works.

The writer already knows all his characters. Most often the characters come to the writer as part of the conception; more precisely, the most common source of concepts is that the writer is attracted first to the character because of something dramatic the character has done, or which it is possible or likely for the character to do. In history and biography, and in all the best fiction, character and story are inseparable. In belles-lettres the character in question is most often that of the author – an interestingly questionable character in a large number of cases.

In cases where the concept comes to you as an abstract, you must go looking for your characters but this is not quite the mechanical task it sounds, because they are there, simply undiscovered at this point. Taking an example at random from the news today, 3 July 1989: the Supreme Court in Washington has today handed down a judgement which returns important legislative rights in the matter of abortion to the States; the Justices warn that this does not affect *Roe v Wade 1973*, and the general assumption is therefore that the principle of abortion will again come before the Court. This is an opportunity for a writer and you grab it. Now, it so happens that one of the Justices is actually a woman, which would make the disguising job a bit difficult – but surely, in a story about a woman's right to control of her own body, with overtones of motherhood and other matters intimately known to women, a woman judge with a swing vote (precisely the case in real life, incidentally) is an obvious character, possibly the leading character. So are two males judges, one conservative, one progressive, perhaps as important leads, perhaps as symbols of the social divisions they represent. So are the campaigners on both sides and the lawyers pleading their cases. Any or all of these might be major or minor characters, depending on where you see your story from: if your concept is to deal with the abstract principle of privacy and individual rights made flesh, you might with profit concentrate on the Court and its people and procedures; if you choose to present your story from the viewpoint of, say, the rape-victim on whom society is forcing an unwanted child, the establishment figures will be seen from your main character's very different perspective and will therefore *be different people*. But the characters are already in place, just waiting for you to perform the mental exercise of pulling them from a news report and from your subconscious, according to how you visualise your concept and the tone of voice you will adopt. If you cannot make an immediate choice, make a list of the characters and ask yourself with whom you can most easily identify; those will be the characters with whom you can most easily help your readers identify, and they will determine your tone of voice.

111

Two women friends reading this passage say: 'You don't have to look for your main character or your story. It is the threat under which the woman Justice sells out,' and 'I agree, but your very human story is how a woman of liberal politics can take a stand on the sanctity of life even under intolerable pressure from her own people to do the fashionable thing.' A male writer with a newspaper background says, 'Maybe, but for the genuine human touch I'd start with the little people in Mississippi or Missouri, and work my way up from there with the [Supreme] Court as the climax, seen from the viewpoint of the people most affected. Who cares about what happens inside the head of some Olympian Supreme Court Justice? Will readers believe you can ever adequately explain such people? No. Those state legislators, and the pressure groups who worked on them – readers are a lot closer to understanding them, and to believing that you're taking them [readers] right into their homes and hearts and minds.' There are in this paragraph at least four different concepts, and consequently as many different main characters, suitable for a current affairs book, history in the making. If the given facts inspire fiction, the possibilities are limitless.

Vital alterations Characters in the subconscious come from your family, your friends, your workmates, the printed and electronic news, and fiction and non-fiction. Not all of the stored information is of the same consistency. Your mind may have glimpsed the florid face of a bus driver and stored it until just the right moment, when you will stick it on a business executive; meanwhile your mind will have made lateral closures between the face and, perhaps, eating habits, dress, the man's sex life, his insurance agent's fears.

Whatever comes from your mind is normally already so filtered that, if you cannot recall a source, you are probably in the clear. If you can recall a source, you must make enough changes to ensure that the character in your book does not bear enough resemblance to the character in real life to support an action for libel or plagiarism. A pig-faced

112

bus driver whom you never met, never spoke to, but depict as a bus driver may bring an action for libel if he can prove he is a regular driver on your route. If you want to use his face, use it on a character not even Edward de Bono, the prophet of Lateral Thinking, could connect with the profession of bus driving. In the cutting and rewriting you will make further distancing changes, and these are normally your guarantee against libel actions even when you cannot remember the source. Believe me, there *is* a source somewhere in your subconscious. I mentioned in *Writing a Thriller* that, after searching my memory conscientiously, I recalled three men called Quentin who all hated their names and after whom the mountaineering hero in my disaster novel *Sinkhole* had been named. Since then my memory has unearthed five other men named Quentin whom I also knew before I wrote the novel, none of whom are overly happy with the name. It is impossible to stress enough how careful you must be about libel.

Theft or homage? Professional writers do not normally admit that they take some of their characters from the writings of their peers. They may not know themselves that they do this, because the source is, as we have seen, disguised by the subconscious, and the material mutated in the same place. The practice is implicitly recognised by the joke that if a beginner 'borrows' from another writer it is plagiarism but when a famous writer 'borrows' it is homage. Theoretically one should be able to avoid the practice in fiction, but the theory falls flat if you agree with me that in real life the transfer is both involuntary and unconscious. In non-fiction the practice may be unavoidable: your brand new interpretation of some of Eisenhower's actions may depend totally on drawing out clearly the morality instilled in him in his Abilene childhood which, as we know, is not in itself a new idea. In practice it is what you make of an idea that gives your writing freshness, not whether it is original. Sir Isaac Newton, asked the source of his genius, gestured at the books in his library and said, 'I stood on the shoulders of giants.'

Plagiarism In fiction you should not without permission take the name of a character, or copy his characteristics, directly from another writer's book. That is plagiarism and theft of intellectual property. Even if the number of possible plots is limited, variation is easily come by because different characters will carry each plot in different directions. In practice, the determination of theft of intellectual property turns almost invariably not on the plot but on the characterisation because it is the characters who give the plot its distinction. Everyone knows that published words are copyright but characters are also protected under copyright and trademark laws as intellectual property. You cannot write a novel with James Bond as a character unless you first come to an arrangement with the literary executors of the estate of the late Ian Fleming (an unlikely event because John Gardner has already been chosen).

To avoid accusations of plagiarism in non-fiction, even when dealing with the agreed facts sourced from secondary material, you should draw on several sources instead of only one. Direct quotes should be attributed; your conclusions should either be original or freshly stated in your own words or, if merely a compendium of the quoted conclusions of others, properly attributed.

Creating a character from scratch Despite what we agreed above, the occasional character is created from more or less thin air, but, unless born for a walk-on part, such characters are too dangerous to the whole of the book to dally with very often. What happens is that during the writing you have a sudden need for a character, say a supercilious bank manager. You are concentrating hard on your story but your own current bank manager is the soul of tact and charm and you honestly cannot now remember any movies in which the bank manager was supercilious. You have nothing to work with. The correct thing to do is to make a note to complete the passage later and to carry on working on the next section; when you have finished the rest of the book you can return and spend the necessary time inventing the bank manager, by which time you will find your subconscious probably offers you thirteen supercilious stiff suits of which one is certain to fit the bill.

The problem with best-case advice is that some of us have Teutonic souls. We finish what we start; we are proud of it: Caligula had his immovable rigour. This problem with the unforeseen need for a minor character, a supercilious bank manager, happened to me. It stopped me dead and wasted days while I wrote him over and over – and every time he came out cardboard. When, under deadline pressure, I chucked him in and continued with the rest of the book, the moment the last page was finished, there was my baker's dozen of supercilious bank managers and twenty minutes later the job was done, the two pages that had cost a fruitless week written to perfection. The experience is akin to forgetting someone's name: the more pressure that is brought to remember the name, the less likely it is that you will; but the moment the pressure is lifted you will certainly remember with renewed clarity.

You should not create a major or minor character or even a key cameo from scratch by tailoring him precisely to the need of a plot you have already worked out; the process works only with the most minor of characters and then not invariably – and critics delight in picking on writers who do not pay as much attention to their most minor creations as to the hero and heroine. Characters bigger than a walk-on created from scratch to the dictates of the plot will wreck your book because the publisher will instantly understand that plot drives character, instead of character driving plot; such books, in the unlikely event of finding publication, convince no readers of the author's authority because that depends on the reader's identification with the character and the reader will not identify with a cardboard character. The reader may be a limp wimp himself, but in his heart he knows it's because of his unique character flaws, not because god created a plot that called for a limp wimp and then die-stamped him. In practice, the plot peopled with characters created for no other purpose than to fill the bus seems improbable even when it is, objectively to another pro, a good plot; in contrast, real characters can make even

115

genuinely stupid plots credible. This seems incredibly unfair to the beginner, who can pick great plots out of his paper every morning but finds the concept of character as motivation for whole books, as well as the process of driving the tangible plot with the intangibles of character, to be infuriatingly imprecise in definition and hard to achieve in practice; it is little consolation that this is a stage everyone one has to go through on the way to becoming a professional writer. If you try hard enough and long enough, one day the problem will simply no longer be there, disappearing between one writing session and the next without apparent reason, which is why it is so helpful in the beginning to take the primacy of character as an act of faith, so that even before you achieve full understanding you can reap some of the great benefits available to those who have mastered character. In fact, one sometimes wonders if full conscious understanding is possible. A writer's understanding of character might well be akin to that of the master cabinetmaker who, asked what he felt when he ran his hand over the grain of a block of wood, pointed to a fine finished cabinet and said, 'Like that, only more so.' Saul Bellow talks of characters 'declaring independence' and that too rings the same bell with many writers.

A small taste We have already quoted from Andrew McCoy's novel *Small War, Far Away*. This extract depicts a dinner hosted by Lance Weber and Tanner Chapman for the gross lawyer Hector Matos, a minor character who here makes his only physical appearance, and who has already disposed of a whole duck at this, his second meal of the evening:

> The fillet the waiter slid in front of the lawyer was fully seven inches across and five high. 'Good god, you're not going to eat that, are you?' said Tanner.
> 'And a zabaglione made with a dozen large brown eggs to compensate for a poor Italian dish I had earlier tonight,' Matos instructed the waiter. 'Then put a nice one-pound Brie on the side of the stove for me. And

ask the sommelier to bring us two more bottles of the '59 Krug. My dear Tanner, around this time I always have a little something, or didn't you read Christopher Robin when you were a boy?'

'"A little pot of honey",' Lance quoted from memory.

'Yes sir,' said the waiter, writing, stunned into obedience by awe of Matos' greed, 'a little pot of honey for you.' He looked enquiringly at Tanner. 'And for you, sir?'

Even the waiter, who is not otherwise particularised, is made memorable by his reaction to Matos. And the reader, when he later hears Matos' voice on the telephone, is not likely to be distracted from the story by casting around for a physical image to attach to the lawyer: he has already been given one that will stick. The writer, having built a mini-portrait to inspire awe, then as much as tells the reader, through the waiter, that he should stand in awe.

Compound characters Many of the mind's creations are simple compounds or, to use Mr Bellow's nomenclature again, composites. The writer sticks on his character a face he has observed on a train, the posture of a body seen in a meeting with a client, a mannerism dredged from the fog of ancient memory without father or mother, a snobbery of dress garnered from an advertisement. In cases of doubt, he should do it consciously for his self-protection, as we have seen, but in most cases the creative process of the mind has done it; the character springs forth, like Athena from the helmet of Zeus, ready to shape the plot. It is however a good exercise to attempt to understand what happens. If you attend a writers' group, or a creative writing tutorial, it could be immensely instructive, as well as entertaining, to ask everyone to bring to the next meeting a single character, described perhaps on a single page, that could be said to represent the group, to be a synthesis of it; the character may be described in action if desired. In other words, ask the members of the group each to create a stereotype by

117

reduction from characteristics that can be observed within the group. Note that no points are given for accurate observation (something we can safely leave to lesser writers). The trick is to analyse the returned characters one by one – note that the writer is not required to justify any or all of his creation and that a strong discussion leader is necessary to avoid descent to destructive personalities – and see how little of the most convincing characters is actually recognisable even when you have deliberately identified the source material in advance. If you give this exercise a second cycle, allowing the participants to take their studies away for another week to rewrite them, the very best writers in your group will probably turn in characters that are absolutely unrecognisable even to their direct progenitors.

How plot flows from character In an early draft of my novel *Festival,* the hero, Bruce Ransome, was an Englishman. But nobody was prepared to believe that an Englishman, charged with the running of a big state-funded arts festival, would assist a Russian conductor to defect. Everyone believed that he would expect the government to do the job, especially since he was friendly with the boss-politician. The moment he was changed to an American, my and his credibility gap as regards his ruggedly individualistic action went away; what is more, the rest of his actions were instantly more organically unified, seemed more of a piece, more in line with what we knew of his character, less startling and therefore more believable.

This is not a rare example of a character being created or changed to fit a plot and surviving. At the time the only Britishers I knew well were American-educated, shared American mores, and worked with me in high-pressure international business – they were self-starters who had skipped a sinking island as soon as they could (this was before Mrs Thatcher's miracle) and were in all but birth Americans. In truth, Ransome was created an American and mislabelled. The moment he was relabelled correctly, the actions that followed from his unique character moved from the realm of the fantastically improbable into that of the only too frighteningly possible. It was this experience which first turned my intellectual belief in the primacy of character as the creator of credible and involving narrative into an abiding faith.

Because character and plot in any good book are so intricately intertwined, it is difficult to analyse the work of another writer, and dangerous if he is still alive because he might pop up to contradict the impertinence. But it does seem that in Tom Sharpe's hilarious comedy *The Throwback* the driving force behind the entire plot, in the sense of the actions of all the main characters, is the illegitimacy of the protagonist, and the main drive of the chief character, Lockhart Flawse, is his perception of this illegitimacy. It would be easy to type the plot as Lockhart's search for his father, which would no doubt give Mr Sharpe a giggle as he is prone to setting traps for unwary analysts and critics, but in fact the majority of the action is inspired not by the search (which is a red herring never addressed in earnest even if rib-ticklingly concluded) but by Lockhart's *reaction* to the restrictions his illegitimacy place upon him. For instance, because he has no birth certificate, he cannot draw welfare and, in retaliation, when he becomes rich he refuses to pay taxes and defends his home ingeniously against the depredations of the taxmen. Lockhart's reaction is predictable from the moment we are told that he was brought up in isolation to believe in those tenets Victorian England held dear: straight shooting, an eye for an eye, and if possible self-enrichment in the process. This is the fictional equivalent of Eisenhower's Abilene childhood, which colours the rest of his life. Lockhart's character creates those situations that in Mr Sharpe's elegant descriptions cause staid solicitors in first class commuter carriages to laugh aloud. With all due respect to Mr Sharpe's genius, no writer could have conceived such situations without first creating such a character to inspire them.

Let us, before our luck runs out, pick on a writer who can't hit back. Do you think it is possible Shakespeare sat down and said, 'In this battle scene a spot of light relief would not come amiss, so let me invent Falstaff, a gross old greedy coward'? It is obviously an absurd idea. No, the posturing, pusillanimous Falstaff, the ever more priggish Prince Hal, all the others, were obviously already present in Shakespeare's mind before he started work, so that, when he came to the battle scene, the comic sequence which makes all the rest so much more terrifying followed from the availability of the fat knight and his weakness of character, already shaped in Shakespeare's mind. Shakespeare's genius has nothing to do with plot – he lifted that straight from the pop historian Holinshed – but with his mastery of character. All Shakespeare's universality and humanity is due to his command of credible characters. Where even Shakespeare comes closest to failing is when his plot threatens to overwhelm his characters, as in *Coriolanus*. It is instructive, if you have the time, to work through the writings of a great writer like Shakespeare and see how different – and perhaps less great – his work would have been without those small touches that arise from the actions of lesser characters. At the same time, note how the characters always act in character; a good parlour game is to guess at what history would have been if great leaders had different personalities – for instance if Churchill had been a wimp who surrendered to Hitler...

Creating living characters The first thing to grasp about character, personality, call it whatever you will, is that in real life no one understands it perfectly; a lot of fascinating writing in psychology and psychiatry belongs less to science or even philosophy than to speculative literature and many of the leading thinkers in the field would be less famous if they did not write such fine prose. It is only writers who play god and pretend they have plumbed the secret of character perfectly. All the same the truly perfect character, without any rough edges, is a dime-store Indian and good only for firewood. Like the too-perfect plot, the perfect character does not sit easily with readers, who themselves suffer only too painfully from human failings. The problem is usually compounded in that perfect characters generate perfect plots (remember, we have already dismissed the perfect plot peopled with specially created 'perfect' characters as a stillborn abomination). The easiest way to ensure that your characters have a dimension of humanity recognisable to readers is to allow them some small failing. Note 'allow', not 'give': this is not a planning matter; instead, when the character reveals himself in the writing complete with a small failing, do not strike it out in an effort to perfect him. Perfect self-knowledge in a character is one of the more irritating errors perpetrated by new writers. An imperfect self-knowledge on the part of a character can be very appealing and tell the reader a great deal about the character; it is also likely to be mistaken for 'character development' by the tackier kind of critic. In this extract from Andrew McCoy's *Small War, Far Away*, the writer turns the trap into an advantage when Lance Weber sees for the first time the child that was born while he was in court being acquitted of a murder charge.

[The baby] looked up and Lance noticed it had the smooth olive skin of its mother but the eyes he looked into every morning while he shaved. He was not a man to think of himself much, but when he did he considered himself a warm person with human frailties. Looking into the already intelligent but coolly appraising eyes of his child, he discovered with shock how others must sometimes see him.

A related matter is the impetus of evil. No one over the age of five, except the mentally disturbed, practices evil for its own sake. There must be some other motive: revenge on persons or society, gain or greed, sensation-seeking, jealousy or envy, whatever, even straightforward weakness in the face of circumstances (though the pity created by this in readers is difficult to handle for the inexperienced writer). That there is a reason for evil deeds is important especially in the creation of credible bad guys.

Nor is the credible character perfectly consistent. If you knew someone in real life who was perfectly consistent, or nearly so, he would probably be your least favourite person precisely for his inflexibility. When we speak of a character 'acting in character' what we mean is that his actions must be predictable; even if they are startling, they must be explicable in terms of what we have seen of his character so that the readers says, not, 'He'd never do that,' but, 'Why didn't I think of that?' Predictability and consistency are, for our purposes here, not the same thing. Whatever small inconsistency your character has would bring with it its own predictability of those actions inspired by that area of his character, which might then be opposed to the predictable actions inspired by his preponderant characteristics; this internal friction is a major cause of your and my love for the characters of great fiction because it makes it easier for us to identify with them. In practice heroes and heroines are usually saved from offensive perfection and incredible consistency by a single small double-purpose character-flaw which, considering how much time the main characters spend on stage, sooner rather than later makes its appearance on the principle of familiarity breeding contempt; at the rewriting stage you should check for its presence. The danger lies more in making baddies black all the way through, but all you can do is to watch out for this in the writing and make alterations if you see trouble approaching or, more often, after the event when you discover the problem in the rewriting stages.

Character names One of your first planning sheets should be a list of the names of your characters. Write any names inherent in the concept on your list. Before you can start writing, you should add a certain minimum of information about appearance, age, pertinent habits. That is all the planning required and more is counterproductive. A page or two should suffice to list all your major characters with their brief descriptions, and the names of all your minor characters. More than the bare minimum is a waste because the art of characterisation lies more in drawing strands from your memory and subconscious than in physically creating anything from scratch, a process better applied at its proper place in the writing of your book than in isolation.

There is also the consideration that character is better created in action rather than in mere description. By his deeds shall we know the character. Writing character notes or extended descriptions extraneous to the action of the book is therefore a waste of time.

All this is not an argument for having *no* list of characters. There is a small but common block suffered by many writers, the momentary inability to remember the name of a character. Having to break the flow of your work to find his name in your earlier writing can be disastrous. However, if you have a short list beside your typewriter, you can glance at it and have your memory refreshed in an instant that does not distract or interrupt.

Though in general your characters get no specific allocation of your time (because in fact they get all your time though it is called by other names) it is worth spending as much time as is necessary specifically on the names of your characters. A powerful American editor told me he could not read all of most of the books he bought but he made a point of reading the opening pages and then checking the odd page here and there for the character names because appropriately named characters is one infallible sign of the professional author. Names have power: in Africa one can find tribes where everyone has at least three names: one for outsiders, one for family and very close friends, one between themselves and their god which, if discovered by enemies, can be used to destroy them.

First of all, unless you are writing comedy, farce, satire or parody, do not give your characters joke-names or clever-clever names. Lockhart Flawse, whom we met above, would be marginal outside those limits except perhaps in a romantic novel – and his creator makes the requisite detour into slush-land – but in the beginning Tom Sharpe sets him up so tightly against his Northumbrian background, where such a name might well be not only possible but common for all we know, that it is only when he draws our attention to the romantic possibilities of the name that we catch on. Getting away with that kind of thing takes a great deal more skill than most novices possess and, anyway, Mr Sharpe works in the right medium for it, comedy. Recently a romance set in the antebellum South caused me to burst out laughing on discovering that the hero's name was Oak; after that it was impossible for the writer to recover my trust and I flung the thing away after about twenty pages. Choosing the right names underscores a publisher's faith in your good judgement. No fewer than three editors queried the name given to the mercenary soldier in *Reverse Negative*, Colonel Stormgood, and I now regret my insistence on keeping the name.

Secondly, if names have power, some names must obviously be more powerful than others and you should choose your character names accordingly. Names are words and the power of words arise from their associations. Ian Fleming's James Bond: a bond is strong, trustworthy. Charles McCarry's Paul Christopher: a good man who stands by his principles. Le Carré's George Smiley: an agreeable fellow but down to earth. Pasternak's Lara: for me she will never by anything but lyrical and unattainable. The same applies to bad guys. Dr Mabuse: obviously a child beater. Dr Strangelove: without doubt a weirdo and a pervert. Theodore Bruun: incontestably a bully and a thug. Jonas Wilde: a strong manly sound with overtones of the unexpected – he turns out to be an assassin who kills with his hands. Some names have a particular currency in the public mind that is too strong for mere authors to buck. Don't name your heroine Marilyn unless you intend her to be a tragic whore. Don't name her Marilyn, Judy, Edith or Maria if she is a tragic whore who commits suicide unless it would be useful promotion for your book to have the women's movement climb all over you – try Camilla instead and for suicide substitute a wasting disease and you might luck into some critical mileage from the poseurs. Carmen is a perfectly common name in Spanish-speaking countries but 44 out of the 50 English-speakers we tested envision any woman called Carmen as overweight, overdressed and overpaid, looking very much like an opera-singer in full stage get-up. While on the subject of women's names, the only Gladyses I know are distinctly upper-class and one is an aristocrat, but the general public, and Americans in particular, seem to think it is a name for serving-girls.

It pays to remember that America is the biggest market, but the rest of the English-speaking world (the so-called Traditional British Market) is the second biggest. The tone of your book is obvious in your choice of names before the reader has read more than a paragraph and if a reader is in doubt whether Hilary or Evelyn or Auberon is a man or a woman (they are all three male writers called Waugh), you have stopped him while he works it out, you have prevented him from carrying on with your story, which is what he is most interested in, you have planted the first seed of doubt in your authority, and you have offered him a chance and temptation to put your book aside.

PROBLEM CHILDREN

We have now finished with the 'above the line' character considerations, which are those that (like characterisation and development) you do not give conscious thought because you expect they will work themselves out in the writing, or that (like libel and choice of names) are given conscious thought as a planning procedure. There remains a number of aspects of character which demand conscious attention because they stop you in the writing or catch your eye in the cutting and rewriting cycle.

If you are stopped in the writing, the best advice is to make a note in the margin and pass on to the next paragraph or section, returning to solve the problem when the rest of the manuscript is complete. It is tough to follow this advice but any other procedure wastes tremendous amounts of time, as in my example of the supercilious bank manager above.

Hey, garçon It is prudent to have a list of unallocated character names somewhere on your desk so that the minor characters your major characters meet can be instantly named, if they need naming, without holding up the writing.

The convention is that non-speakers are never named and

that minor characters with lines are named only if necessary. Exceptions to this rule in literature that has stood the test of time are so plentiful that it is probably fair for us to question its wisdom. First, it conflicts with another, if more modern convention, which says that the writer enhances his authority by particularising everything: the hero doesn't just take the plane to Russia, he takes the Japanese Airlines flight JAL 733 leaving Frankfurt at 9.41pm for Sheremeteyevo Airport, Moscow, where it is scheduled to land at 1.18am but is usually kept in pattern for another nine-and-a-half minutes because when there aren't military overflights the Russians make all other airlines run late out of sheer bloodymindedness. Secondly, the names of minor characters can add instant flavour to a milieu. On that JAL flight, the name Kyoko on the stewardess' nameplate is an inexpensive touch of colour, and if the hero uses it an instant way of showing that he relates easily to people, even inscrutable orientals. American writers seem not to realise that it is a cliché to show their characters as regular guys by having them joke with bellhops and car jockeys, and Americans in general fail to understand that it is not a character reference that barmen – barmen! – around the world greet one by name, but that is the world we live in and the writer, unless he can afford to do without airport sales, cannot buck the trend. However, you must not take this naming beyond the bounds of credibility. In an army officers' mess, for instance, it would be infra-dig for an officer or guest to know the barman's name: he's 'Barman' or 'Corporal' or 'Sergeant' – yes, including every American mess I have ever been in. And, while we're on the subject of American egalitarianism: whatever American movies tell you (perhaps naively, but more probably because that is what the official armed services adviser, who controls the men and machines lent to the production at taxpayers' expense, wants them to tell you), in the armed services officers and non-commissioned ranks and enlisted men are not on first-name terms across these ferocious class barriers. Thirdly, a handle like 'the doorman' if used repeatedly is dull when you can give the character a monicker like 'Kelly'

126

which at least tells your audience he is Irish so that the reader can imagine his few words to be spoken in brogue even if you don't say so or, if Kelly has no lines, at least imagine him to have a stereotype Irish face. There are objections to this. There is no such thing as an 'Irish face'. But, if you want to give your reader the benefit of closures in the mind, you must give him something to hang associations on. The name of the character is the least space-consuming method. Kowalski would definitely be a different doorman from Kelly, wouldn't you say?

Character v. pace A point *may* come in the writing where you might feel that you are building character at the expense of pace. A point *will* come in the cutting and rewriting cycle when you will see that you have built character at the expense of pace. If neither point arises, you have skimped the job. Even leathery old pros, who know in their bones exactly how much to write, always find something to cut to enhance the pace. But you do not have their experience and you need guidance.

It follows directly from our emphasis on character as the benevolent fountainhead that you should *write for character and cut for pace*. Therefore, *always* when writing give the space and benefit of doubt to characterisation and *always* when cutting and rewriting give the benefit of doubt to pace and make the cut. You can always come back and cut, but it is extremely tiresome to go back to extend characterisation because it is both time-consuming and difficult for the writer to recover the mood of the characters at that point in the story's development where he now discovers the characterisation to be thin. It is one reason historians and biographers, with all the facts at their fingertips and theoretically capable of starting work anywhere at all, still prefer writing in chronological order, because the reactions of the men and women who determine their events are shaped by prior events.

So, while writing, don't give pace more than a passing thought. Concentrate instead on what your characters think, do and say, and why. Drive for show and putt for the money.

Dull characters There are boring plots aside from those of the 'new wave' writers but they are the result not of malice but of incompetence in creating and controlling characters, so need not concern us except as examples from which we can learn how not to succeed. With proper command of characters, no plot need be boring, given that there is even the slightest story to tell.

However, you may find in your book the need for boring characters. In all but fiction the requirement for some kind of objective truth, or at least the appearance of it, demands a rounded view. If your subject had a boring politician or general as his confidante, or in the next cell, or if you're a travel writer escorted around China for three months by a humourless government official, you will have to indicate this somehow without boring the reader. Unlike Elmore Leonard you cannot 'leave out the boring bits readers always skip'. But you can reduce their number and length: 'Han Dung Yi was such a humourless, dried-up old stick that we did our best to ignore his glowering presence. We soon learned that if we spoke to the common people for long enough, they would, after a while, forget his presence. The thing was to hang on until they got used to him.' Mention the bore, or the dullard, or the slow-witted, or the beetle-browed, or whoever holds up the action, and then ignore him until he again forwards the story.

It is, unfortunately, not true that fiction writers can skip the dull bits, whatever Elmore Leonard may claim, though one sometimes wishes all of them would try as hard as Mr Leonard does to be courteous to their readers. It may be that your story contains its less than exciting characters, and often the dull character or two, who are essential to the plot or as foils for the other characters. Note that 'essential to the plot' which often accounts for their dullness; if they are created to satisfy some plot-purpose they are by definition damned and you must start again on them. Those created as foils, major or minor, will not serve even that purpose unless they are created in the same way as all other good characters, because the necessary friction arises only between real characters. (One teacher of writing has two

128

very worn supermarket point-of-sale figures he rubs together to make the point that 'cardboard cutouts create no heat'. Precisely!)

That leaves us with the dull character who is correctly created – and therefore all the more likely to be *very* boring in a quite small space – and cannot be cut because he is essential to the story. All you can do is make him spatially as small as possible. For instance, show the garrulous character in full flow for a longish paragraph to give the reader the flavour of the boredom he induces, then cut away to other action before cutting back to the bore with a summary: 'And still Bill spluttered on. And on. And on.' When we see Bill again, a summary reminder will suffice: 'Bill was there, talking, talking, talking. Both of us avoided him.' The alternative is to send the dull person up – but comedy is only for the genuinely gifted and skilled, in other hands too easily going over the top and being merely ridiculous and intensely destructive of the rest of your work.

A word of warning: I speak here of dull characters for whom you, as a writer, feel the same sympathy or antipathy as you would as a person out and about in society, and as you feel for the exciting characters. Characters who are dull because you the writer, standing in for you the person, are simply indifferent to them, will always be dull, are impossible to save and should be chucked out. There is no such thing as a character to whom the writer is neutral (as distinct from being indifferent, not the same thing at all), though sometimes we pretend otherwise; this applies to non-fiction as much as fiction. If the character gives you no buzz, for or against, what's he doing in your book?

Baddies All writers, no matter how experienced, need to pay special attention to their black hats, in the first instance because they receive less space than the heroes for character development and are therefore more easily pushed over the edge into caricature.

The quickest way to turn a baddie into a joke is to make him entirely consistent, evil right through. It should follow that the easiest way of making him real, and perhaps even giving him a modicum of the reader's sympathy which in turn will enhance the friction between characters and the tension of the story, is to allow him some inconsistency. 'He might be black rock all the way round but if you break him you will find *Mother* engraved on his heart in purest white,' as offered in another manual as an example of 'variegation', is not inconsistency but an entirely consistent sentimentality shared by the whole fraternity of violent criminals, on the same level as the assassin who loves cats. We believe in the bitchy lady who loves cats, because they have not rejected her for her sharp tongue as people have, but most readers recognise the assassin's love for cats as an insulting artifice dreamed up by a careless writer. Because the inconsistency must not be obviously fake, and cannot be so important relative to his dark side as to turn the bad guy into a good guy, in practice adding inconsistency to the character of the baddie is a second choice.

The first choice is flawed rationality and my own preferred way is to make the hero sympathise with the bad guy's plight but abhor his methods of seeking redress. For instance, a hero can make a calmly reasoned, compassionate argument for righting the wrongs suffered by the Catholics in Northern Ireland, or the Palestinians in Israel, but conclude that neither justifies the bad fellow's terrorism which, philosophically, must always be aimed at undermining all other more or less democratic processes of adjustment in favour of the absolutism of the terrorist leaders. Or, more simply, the hero can agree with the baddie's green politics yet prevent him causing a nuclear explosion in downtown New York to publicise his concern. An advantage of this method is that your hero can have it both ways without seeming hypocritical or mawkish.

There are other ways of doing the same job but none of them work as well for novices as my first and second choices, and most, like telling the baddies' story unblinkingly from their viewpoint as if they are 100 per cent in the right and entitled to the reader's sympathy (described in detail in my how-to book *Writing a Thriller* with an extended example in my novel *Reverse Negative*), are in the wrong circumstances dangerous in the hands of the unpractised.

Runaway characters Though it is common and indeed desirable and essential for your characters to 'declare independence' from the source of their creation, and to a good extent from any bonds your formal planning might put on them, because otherwise your readers will not believe in them, a case arises known as the 'character running away with the author'. There are no genuine cases known to me of this happening to a professional author, and in every case I have experience of where it happened to an aspirant the problem was caused by autobiographical material growing and growing until it overpowered everything else. Reduced to essentials, the problem arises from a lack of discipline in not spotting a self-indulgence and circumscribing it very strictly. The answer is to finish writing the book, read it to see how terrible it is, put it away and to start immediately on something else which should not be autobiographical. After a space, probably years rather than months, you can return to the subject material of the first book, preferably without reading it again, and make a fresh start in the light of experience gained in the books completed in the meantime.

Over the top? How can you know when your characters are over the top? Consider this: could it be that Tom Sharpe in the beginning had set out to write a long-faced novel on serious philosophical and literary issues (all his novels turn on such points when one reduces them to common denominators), decided on finishing it that his characters were over the top, and put it away sadly until a friend pointed out it was in fact high comedy? Of course nothing of the sort happened but it is not an impossible or even improbable scenario.

Correctly created characters can, because they act in character, by definition never be over the top. Our handle must then be the situations the characters' actions land them in: if these seem over the top, it is because they are not well-motivated, at which point it is a simple matter to go back along the chain and find the broken link, usually caused by a character who is overly consistent – too good, rotten all the way through – so that we do not believe in his humanity and therefore fail to believe in any situation he causes. Mr Sharpe is chosen as an example because his situations are truly outrageous, yet we believe in them because they result directly from the peculiarities of his characters.

The 99 per cent solution By now you should be taking on board an important point, which is that the very large majority of a writer's problems are caused by the failure of his character-creation. Whenever you run into a problem you should look first to your characters for the cause and also for a solution. Furthermore, there is no reason to panic when you get it wrong. Character creation is not a mystical art; it is a simple craft learned by repeatedly making minor improvements to your existing skill until you make a major breakthrough and it becomes second nature to you to consider character first, last, and always.

We have now arrived at what in tennis is called break point. For the writer this is the point where you have your complete first draft to hand and put the manuscript aside for at least six months* – or as long as it takes to finish the first draft of another book if that is longer – to gain the perspective of time on your writing before you start work on the cutting and rewriting that will complete the game. Start on your next book immediately, or after a break of a week or two, no more, because otherwise the essential habitual routine of writing will be broken.

---

*Except the writer who follows the John Braine Memorial Method, who starts work on his second and potentially final draft almost immediately.

7
MURDERING
DARLINGS
CUTTING AND REWRITING

'LEARN that time will sort the good from the bad, including your own bad,' Doris Lessing advises young writers. This is the verdict of history we have already brought into our deliberations. This chapter is about methods by which an author can give that verdict a gentle nudge. The process is called 'cutting and rewriting' or less revealingly 'revising', and describes work done on the first complete draft of a book; in the case of writers following the John Braine Memorial Method, it is often called 'polishing' and describes work done on the complete second draft, the first having been discarded without rewriting. Though in theory the amount of work involved in cutting and rewriting should be less in the Braine Method, in practice it often is not; in any event the procedure is the same. We shall therefore make no further distinction between the two methods of originating a book, appropriating the word 'polishing' for the final gloss applied to your language after all major cutting and rewriting has been done.

THE INITIAL READ-THROUGH

Under no circumstances should you offer your first draft to anyone to read. Only amateurs offer unfinished drafts for opinions – and always hate any honest opinion, which is the only useful kind.

When It is a waste of time to start cutting and rewriting immediately you have finished your first draft (or in the Braine Method your second draft) because you will still be too taken with those of your darlings you will have to murder ruthlessly (Faulkner) to save a publishable book. A mimimum of six months should pass before you even reread what you have written. Nor must you hang around for six months savouring the feeling of being a writer and the anticipation of publication; you must clear your mind totally of the book and the best way is meanwhile to write another complete book. After six months, or on completion of the new book's first draft (which you now in its turn put away to await rewriting when you have not only cut and rewritten the first book, but written a third book's initial draft as well), pull your first book from its drawer and horrify yourself by reading it. You will immediately be struck by how overwritten it is.

What It is a good idea to read a carbon, or, if you have a word processor, a printed copy, on which you can write notes and slash whole sections, paragraphs and sentences even on that first read-through. Always on this initial read-through follow your first, instant instinct. Don't agonise: slash. If it strikes you, its creator, as wrong, it will pass no publisher – and the publisher may not offer you an opportunity to cut, merely a cold rejection slip.

Why Slashing gaily now will save weeks of agonising later. Cutting is the one thing on which even the novice can trust his first instinct: your mind simply won't let you cut beyond the bone.

Of course even a skin-deep cut hurts like hell. But you must cut to the bone or you cannot be published. Publishers and readers interested in felicities of words without any pressure behind them are few and far between and are not the ones with the sort of money that could turn you into a professional writer; even the few interested in fine writing for its own sake are impatient of detours and want the author to take them directly through the main highway of his mind.

How Until now we have been assuming that you write only for yourself, that even if a scene amuses or impresses only you it is better to write it down than to leave it out; certainly we have said that writing insincerely for a market will bring you only grief. But at this point all your genius and sincerity is on the paper. What you must do now is to distil only that part of it which will cause publishers and readers to clasp you to their bosoms and demand that you immediately write more. In cutting and rewriting, therefore, it makes sense to step outside yourself and consider how you would judge the work were you a publisher or reader. Whatever would irritate or confuse or delay a publisher or reader should obviously go.

Where Don't loll about in the sun reading your work. This isn't an occasion for relaxing. Do your cutting and rewriting in the same room and position as you did your writing. It is as serious a venture as the writing, and with much greater consequences.

Where in your manuscript you should start cuttting and rewriting is irrelevant. A great deal will be cut and it doesn't matter where you start. In the end everything will be rewritten.

Do not waste time thinking about the abstract, large issues of cutting and rewriting. When you finish the first reading and rough cut, proceed immediately to the detail-work.

While in everything we have done so far there has been a sound underlying principle for doing things a certain way and in a certain order, often not the most obvious or easiest in the immediate term, in cutting and rewriting practicality rules: there is no abstract reason not to do it the fast, easy way, and the rest of this chapter is presented in the order which causes me the least wasted time in cutting and rewriting my own work. There is no reason you should not experiment if you have the time and the inclination, as long as you perform all the functions and complete all the tasks.

135

CUTTING

Cutting precedes rewriting and proceeds from the large to the small because otherwise you waste time on patching up the detail of work which will end in the bin.

Recognising essentials The correct frame of mind for what follows is that of the tax-collector. You should demand that every word proves its worth beyond question, or you collect it for the dustbin. All questionable cases are saved in the round file. Every word that remains must work for its living and work hard.

On the first read-through you will cut surprisingly large chunks of material as obviously superfluous, even though you will have a firm memory that they seemed very amusing, perhaps even essential, at the time you wrote them. Don't waste time trying to recover the sense of their indispensability. All that counts is whether they make an indispensable contribution to the manuscript as it stands now. What is left should next be checked against your written concept and themes: does the book leave the concept in your mind, are all the important themes fully explicated? Note any which are not but leave the writing of the necessary additional sections until later, merely marking likely places for insertions in the manuscript.

At this rereading, also note any motivations or facts which are lacking and make a note, at the correct place on the manuscript if possible, to attend to the matter in the rewriting stages.

Don't despair if the book is now in a mess, either physical or metaphorical. Patient, disciplined work will sort it out; in this you begin even-steven with every professional writer. You will in any event have to retype the manuscript (and on a wordprocessor virtually every word is also moved around or changed), so that it does not matter if you set to with scissors and paste and vari-coloured ballpoints.

Now start again at the beginning. Can you cut any subplot complete? Ask about each subplot what it contributes to any theme. Is the point not made by another subplot? Or even by simple, acceptable statement by a character? If it is, if it can be, cut it. Check if cutting a subplot does not also allow you to subtract events involving its characters elsewhere.

Can you cut any of the mechanical divisions of your manuscript complete? A book, a part, a chapter, a section between section breaks? Are any of them digressions from the main narrative and, if so, do they contribute anything indispensable to the main narrative or do they serve only to keep the reader interminably from following the main thread in which he is really interested? Any duplications of either action or theme? Cut it: it is boring and readers do not need a made point repeated.

Next check whether it is not possible to combine themes by moving a few paragraphs from one section into another and then cutting the remainder of the first section. If that is possible without damaging the story you should do it, even if in practice it is more onerous or tedious than it sounds in the brisk description here, because the ensuing cut will greatly enhance the pace of the story. Remember, we write for character but we cut for pace.

And pace is our abiding consideration for every other cut we will make.

If you can no longer cut or combine sections, can you cut whole characters? Superfluous characters are the ones who appear only in subplots, or impinge only tangentially on the main characters, or who cause the main characters no reaction at all. Cut them, and their action with them. If you cannot cut a character, can you combine his characteristics with that of another character and so give his action to that character as well? This process creates, as a serendipitous byproduct of doing the job right, lesser characters with memorably split personalities.

Now, let's get down to the nitty-gritty. Read the manuscript again, this time striking every whole paragraph that does not directly contribute to the action in the section. A good test for whole paragraphs is to ask, 'Is the character showing the reader something or am I, the writer, telling the reader something?' The former is legitimate, the latter only rarely even in the non-fiction classes we include here. If the paragraph is recognisably telling rather than showing but cannot be cut for some reason, mark it for rewriting into an acceptable format.

We have several times talked about action without defining it at all closely. Action is the character involved in an event, which may be obviously active, like fighting his make-or-break budget through Cabinet, or merely sitting in a chair thinking – if you can manage to present his thoughts to create friction or tension. What action is not, is the writer telling the reader what happens from some lofty, outside viewpoint, without involvement, an error novices almost always commit. A good test is to see if you can rewrite whatever you want to communicate to the reader as dialogue between characters, or between the character and his conscience: an interior monologue. Regardless of what Nabokov says ('I do not read novels with more dialogue than description'), you cannot have too much dialogue. If what you want to say is not something the character wants to say to another character or to the reader at this place, and you can therefore not rewrite it into action, can he bring himself to say it elsewhere? If not, the probability is that it should go. This is not your story but his. If you cannot manage dialogue or interior monologue, at the very least the paragraph should be rewritten as observation from the vantage point of one of your characters; if this also fails, the assumption must be that it has nothing to do with your characters and you should cut it.

In non-fiction there is an additional question about such a paragraph to be asked before it is cut: is it not simply in the wrong place? Does it not in fact belong to the background chapters setting the scene for the action, where the writer's visibility is more acceptable to readers, rather than here, where it interrupts the flow of the characters' action? If so, and if it does not duplicate information already given, move it; otherwise cut it. 'Meanwhile back in Washington...' is in any event a cliché!

An even less desirable form of the author telling the reader something is authorial comment, or sermonising. You are not Billy Graham. The problem is that the novel is conceptually and traditionally a moral form, though I consider that a matter of choice rather than duty for the modern writer, but your characters' circumstances may make comment or conclusion inevitable. Here Andrew McCoy is unable or unwilling to cut or change the authorial comment beginning 'most of us' in *Lance of God* (Secker & Warburg, London 1987; Grafton, London 1989), perhaps because at that moment his only characters are human corpses and live fieldmice...

> But, again, so many human lives wasted for so many animal lives saved? No, even Christine, who had been fanatical to save the animals, would consider that a fair exchange – most of us would shudder at the very idea: at best, bad taste.

...and instead, after a line space to indicate a break, he steps boldly forward and tells his readers the author is commenting:

> Anywhere else I would not mention this, but in Africa life is a relative matter and this is a story of relativity, though perhaps not all the characters understood that at the time and, of those who survived, at least one would never accept it. That too is human: it is a rare man who, with a rifle in his hand, heeds the warning that a bullet can kill him as easily as anyone else; a Harley Street cancer specialist told me that, of all those he informs they are terminally ill, physicians take the news least stoically.
>
> After this I will not again intrude the person of the narrator. But it is important that you know I put this story together from what participants told me and from what I could guess; I know the area and the people a little. This isn't a god-view: I don't know everything. For instance, who the devil knows what motivates Muamur Qaddaffi? On second thoughts, considering that example, *I don't want to know everything*. I already have my own visions of hell.

After a line space he returns to the story – told in the third person impersonal, the god-view he has just denied! But only the professional critic will notice: Mr McCoy has ingratiated himself for good with every reader by flattering the reader as a literary sophisticate who needs to be apologised to by the author for an almost invisible slip of protocol ('most of us...bad taste'), and topped up his good will by apparently sharing knowing insights about literature, death and politics, plus a couple of modest disclaimers, though he was in fact forwarding a different part of his story for which this allegedly personal detour sets the conceptual frame. Not everyone can put up such a polished performance but that Mr McCoy feels the need to apologise for a very minor breach of literary protocol tells you something of the sophistication and quick reflexes he expects in his mass market audience. He doesn't expect to get away with sermonising in his sixth book, and you shouldn't in your first.

After cutting paragraphs, read the manuscript to strike whole sentences. At this stage it is a good idea to read aloud – many writers speak what they write aloud even as they write the first draft. A key test of a bad sentence is that it is difficult to say aloud in a conversational tone of voice. Strike, or mark it for rewriting. If it doesn't make sense when read aloud (as opposed to merely not sounding conversational) it is worthless and, instead of marking it for rewriting, you can scratch it.

Now read to strike individual phrases and words. Is that qualifying phrase really earning its living, or is it just the writer showing off his objectivity when his character would be too involved to see any but his own side of the question? Is that word really necessary? Will one adjective not do instead of two – in fact, is even one adjective at all necessary?

Permissible indulgences Cutting is especially hard for the novice, who does not yet have the experience that writing the second book is easier than the first, and the tenth very easy indeed. A complicating factor is that many first books, especially novels, have an autobiographical element and asking for massive cuts is like asking Jesus to edit the Gospels to delete all references to himself. There are no permissible indulgences except for those willing to pay the price, which is invariably that they must forgo publication. You can't be a writer without publication.

It is sometimes said that specialised knowledge allows a writer a certain latitude of bad writing but, if this ever was true, it is not the case today. There are simply too many ex-Assistants to the President or jet test pilots or oil advisers to sheiks who can write well, and the stakes are so high that, if they cannot, their books are ghosted. Sorry.

TWO GOOGLIES

So much for method. Cutting is really common sense but there are two specific problems which commonly bother aspirants.

Too much 'establishing' explanation Take any good book off a library shelf and on the first page the author seems to have dropped you in the middle of the action. This is aggravating for the keen novice, whose analysis fails to show how the writer 'just puts the characters there'. There is no mystery about it. The author just starts writing about the key event in the character's life. There is, however, a trick, though it is one you should by now be aware of, and able to use if you put your mind to it. It is letting the character spring full-grown from your mind onto the page, there to develop even further.

This is a matter more of self-confidence than of technique. If you believe you have grasped the essence of the character then it follows that you can start convincingly with the action that follows from his characteristics. Here is the opening sentence from *Mrs Thatcher's Revolution* by Peter Jenkins (Jonathan Cape, London 1987):

> 'I am not a consensus politician...' Margaret Thatcher said, in what was to become her most remembered statement, 'I'm a *conviction* politician.'

The reader immediately wants to know why and how she applies that conviction. The convictions of Mrs Thatcher are central to Mr Jenkins' narrative (and his considerable argument in a book containing much more than historical analysis), so he starts with them. He has thought his case – his case in this instance being Mrs Thatcher's motivation – through well enough to be absolutely certain of carrying his readers with him from the opening line. That's real authority... A lesser writer would have started, perhaps, with Mrs T's girlhood over her father's grocery store, or the failure of will on all sides of British politics that brought her to the fore, but Mr Jenkins, who has, not incidentally, a play to his credit, jumps in with both feet at the key frictional point of her motivation.

In fiction it is actually easier to start right in on the action because you can always come back and establish the background once you have hooked your reader. Undue explanation is often easy to spot by the hoary old test of the writer telling the reader something instead of showing him. If whatever you're telling the reader does not evince itself in the action, the assumption must be that it is unimportant and should be scrapped. If the story is harmed by its removal, mark it for rewriting into action.

There is another kind of 'establishing text', which merely moves the character from place to place, or sets the physical background, as in the movie cliché of the plane taking off and landing, the taxi-ride, the character walking up to a door. Unless they have a purpose, such scenes are entirely skipable. John Braine says quite clearly that no one in fiction should just walk up the stairs: if there is no reason for showing him walking up the stairs, for instance that he meets someone of interest, or that he is reluctant to go into the room at the top of the stairs, then don't show him climbing the stairs, just cut from wherever he is now to the bedroom by saying, 'Upstairs in the bedroom...' Mr Braine's exceedingly, even offensively, simple example is perpetuated here because one still sees this kind of tiresomely superfluous writing even in print, which is presumably also the reason he chose it.

Seamlessness versus the episodic narrative The novice tends to worry about something the pro simply ignores, which is that to you and me life is totally sequential because it cannot be anything else, whereas for characters in a book time is chopped into events. The new writer wants to fill in the time in between for the reader. This is not a special case of over-explication but the key to something else. You, as a writer, can never tell the reader everything that happens; your target should instead be to tell the reader everything that is relevant to his understanding of the characters and their actions. Anything more would be boring (and arguments for realism in writing are themselves an infernal irrelevant bore). Instead of seeing this part of our catechism as a restriction which creates a time-chopped narrative, you should view it as an advantage that allows you to create a seamless panoply of cause and effect all in exciting action without tedious description intervening.

REWRITING

Cutting and rewriting is another of those twin-sets we have divided merely for convenience of description. If you see a word that needs changing while you're reading for cutting, of course you should change it. But I would suggest that any rewriting longer than a sentence is merely marked at the appropriate place and put aside until all cuts are finished. Further cuts discovered while rewriting should, however, be made immediately.

Shuffle In fact, the first business of rewriting is to seek further direct cuts, or combinations of material that allow further cuts. This is done by studying your remaining material to see if there is not some way of rearranging its order which will shorten it.

Order and discipline By now you will be overwhelmed by a very tacky stack of pieces of paper. Do not type up a fresh copy before you rewrite – type up the fresh copy *as* you rewrite. If you are working on a word processor, print another hard copy to work on or reformat on screen to a different width (and use a different typeface if you can) to give you a different perspective on the material.

There are advantages to starting at the beginning, and I always do, but you can start anywhere you like as long as you finish each section you start and don't hop around, which is a recipe for confusion and disaster.

First, write all additional material you have noted is required for expounding your themes in full. Second, write all additional linking action required to ensure all actions are fully motivated. Third, add all pieces where you have noted the need for research, and have executed the research as described in the next chapter. Now reread the whole thing to check that the chain of motivation is complete – and to discover what else you can cut in the light of the additional material.

Next rewrite all paragraphs marked in your various readings as being capable of tightening. Rewrite all sentences that are not instantly clear and can absolutely not be cut.

Rewrite the complete first chapter or section in the light of your newly enhanced skills; the opening will be the most important part of your work in the process of selling it. Check the ending and rewrite if necessary – more often than not it will be fine. Now work through the book again and consciously check every sentence for superfluous and imprecise words. At the same time check that every sentence is as clear as possible: it should say only what you intend it to say without undertones or overtones you do not intend. A final reading should check once more for possible cuts and tightening up of words and meaning, and serve to ensure that after all the cuts and shuffling the hooks and starts are still in place and connect correctly.

Trapezoids At this stage a problem often manifests itself. We seek clarity in our structures of construction (plot, characterisation, placement of breaks) and in our detailing right down to word-level, of which the paradoxical result is that clarity of meaning comes into conflict with comprehensibility by the majority. It is known that even educated people regularly use vocabularies of around 800 words though many writers have vocabularies in use of between 3000 and 5000 words depending on who's counting but anyway hugely impressive to the beancounters. Big deal: English has a million words before you even start on jargon, though only about 50,000 of them are certain of finding a place in every general dictionary. We can assume at this late stage that real writers will not use bow-vow words such as 'heuristic' or 'heterogeneous' except perhaps as shorthand in work intended for specialists, nor say 'helot' when we can choose 'slave' or 'helix' for 'spiral' unless there is a special reason. We are trying to communicate, not impress. But what if the only precise word is not common currency? Do you call an area with four unequal sides a trapezoid or do you call it an area with four unequal sides? Many writers believe it an insult to their readers' intelligence not to call it a trapezoid if that is the only precise word but you may have different readers in mind: this is a matter of personal choice. But be certain first that the difficult word *is the only precise word*. Nothing is more tiresome than the writer who displays his vocabulary or linguistic skill only to be exposed, on recourse to a dictionary, to be merely a show-off who scorns plain English for empty pyrotechnics. In a recent Anthony Burgess novel a great many of his Russian words have perfectly good, and in some cases superior, English equivalents, which infuriated this reader, for one.

It is also a courtesy to provide monolingual readers with a translation of foreign sentences used in your text.

Problems with pace Until now, in our cutting and rewriting, we have not consciously considered pace. Pace is a bit like plot, in that it has no independent existence, yet is highly visible in analysis and criticism. However, we have agreed that you should write for character but cut and rewrite for pace. What is this pace? It is the cycle of tension and relief from tension which follows from the reader's identification with the properly motivated actions of correctly drawn characters. The net effect is that pace needs to be considered only when, by its absence, it becomes a problem. In your final reading you should check for pace and, because you will by now be heartily sick of the work, it makes sense to put the manuscript away for several months before doing the final reading prior to seeking a publisher. Note in regard to pace that every book has its own internal pace, not only because it has different characters, but also by reader-expectations in genres. For instance, though most people if pressed can think of genuinely witty books of medium length, the expectation is that witty books will not be long, and farce is generally on the short side, as is pop-biography, whereas romances are hefty.

So, if a lack of pace does manifest itself, how will you fix it? Unfortunately, we are not talking about a 'fix'; we should anticipate, at the very least, a major reshuffle of your material and perhaps, to make the reshuffle work, additional linking passages to be written. This kind of artificial patch-up job might, if everything else is all right, find you publication but everyone will know the book is flawed. The correct way to correct the lack of pace is to rethink the characters because one or more of them, or his/their motivation chain(s), must be flawed; regrettably, you must start at the beginning.

You should also consider that some characters are incapable of pace: I have one manuscript that's been rewritten to the point of nausea and may never make the grade simply because of the leading character's refusal to fit the requirements under which the novel was commissioned: the publisher wanted a sequel to a successful earlier book and wouldn't listen to warnings that ten years on an eighty-year-old hero would be damn nearly comatose, hardly thriller-hero material.

Style, what style? Ernest Hemingway apparently had the style he wished to achieve firmly in his mind from the beginning. We deduce this from his frustrated remark that the critics took for his style those awkwardnesses that stood in the way of fully expressing himself but which he was unable to reduce no matter how hard he tried. Do not weep for poor Ernest. What we are listening to is not an objective self-assessment but the self-pity of perfectionism in its cups. And, as with all nearly great men when *in vino*, the *veritas* is not far beneath the skin: he is telling us in almost so many words that style is nothing more than saying what you wish in the manner you wish.

The message creates the medium. That is right and proper.

We have now reached the end of the decisions that no one else can take for the writer: what and who he writes about, and to a large extent how he writes. What is left is either mechanical or less important than the choices already made. For instance, you may arrange matters so that you never need to do research or you can pay someone to do your research for you; many writers pay an agent a percentage of their income to select publishers for them.

8
BEING PREPARED
RESEARCH

T HE writer in command of his art and his life does as little research as possible. This follows from our belief that the reader is father to the writer, and the writer is an enthusiast for what he writes. Whatever you read for leisure is therefore research; when you are out and about, even just running for exercise, that is in a way research, because whatever you see, whoever you meet, the thoughts in your mind, all are grist to the mill. Remember Saul Bellow saying, 'I didn't start on [*A Theft*]. It just arrived... a windfall'? A young biographer says, 'Well, those diaries and letters were always there. Whenever I had nothing else to do, I read them. One day I was just ready to start work on the book. I hadn't even thought I could really be a biographer until then. I mean, I was going to teach history and this was for me like an extended personal project in local history. No, I hadn't thought of writing to publishers to ask if they would be interested.' Her naïveté embarrasses her deeply; she doesn't quite believe that the majority of books probably originate precisely like hers and are then dressed up in premeditation and volition to make the writers seem smarter than they are. A book of household hints and old saws, not quite within the terms of reference of this book but too striking an example to leave out, came about because my friend Mary Rose Quigg had a noticeboard in her kitchen and kept sticking notes on it for the edification of her daughters and the amusement of her family; every hint and old saw in that book is a labour of love.

As is well known, Frederick Forsyth spends at least six months intensively researching each of his books. One teacher told a creative writing class that Mr Forsythe gets his idea for the book from that research. What an astonishingly unrealistic interpretation. Mr Forsythe, momentary thought would have convinced this teacher, already had his idea – or he would not have known what to research. Len Deighton surely checked every fact in his book on the *Blitzkrieg* with utmost thoroughness, both before and after he wrote it, but the concept for the book would never have arrived if he did not have a pre-existing interest in the Germans and in the military history of that period.

We know that Paul Theroux travels for months on end before he writes a book about his travels. But travels undertaken in Patagonia or across Siberia by train merely as 'research' would reflect the tedium of the journeys. The truth is that Mr Theroux is an inveterate traveller who also happens to be a writer (he's a novelist), so that the book that comes from the journey pays for his passion. One can quite imagine Mr Theroux in the library later, checking a subsidiary fact, such as the correct spelling of an obscure placename. The journey through Patagonia is not research but thinly disguised self-indulgence; the visit to the library is research.

It follows inescapably that the narrative writer, and especially the novice, should do his research after he has written his book, merely to fill in the holes the process of writing exposes.

By contrast, the commissioned book in certain of the classes of prose addressed in this book will have the information-gathering split into four stages, though it is not always obvious which of them are purpose-directed research. The travel book is a good example. Let us say your first travel book on Hadrian's Wall (which, for the sake of argument, is right next to your home) is a success and you tell your publisher over a celebratory lunch that you are fascinated by walks along what used to be the Iron Curtain; he is enthused and a month or six weeks later you have a contract. Part one of the process happened a long time ago:

you were fascinated by those walks and discovered what you could about them to fuel the dream that one day you would go there. Part two happens after your publisher decides there's a book in your dream: in the process of arranging the journey you discover even more, practical details, but this is hardly 'research'. On the walks, you are indulging a hobby, a passion, even if perhaps more systematically than before. Only for tax purposes is this 'research'. Finally you write your book and discover that you did not note this and that relevant fact, or never discovered it because you were enjoying yourself too much, and have to write away for it. That, at last, is research.

A famous and successful professional biographer described to my fledgeling friend how he works. He is commissioned by a publisher, normally to an idea of his own rather than of the publisher ('biography is too personal to stray far from what one knows'), and either already has or is given a mass of archival material in which he then immerses himself until he discovers 'in an instant on rising one morning' that he has 'a complete sense of my subject... in the round against his family and his work', at which stage he starts his first draft which is built either out from, or up to, the 'key revelation of his life'. [This sounds like the political analyst Peter Jenkins, quoted above on Mrs Thatcher, though it is not; judging by results, there might well be some commonality of method.] The first draft is 'not a skeleton but everywhere as full as I can make it'. This draft is then used to discover chronological or motivational gaps in the story ('as a control on the completeness of my material, knowledge and deduction'). Purposeful research, as in attempts to discover paperwork and conducting interviews, is then undertaken, and a second draft written from scratch in the John Braine Memorial Method. It has never happened to this biographer that the additional research to fill in the gaps has caused a fundamental shift in his assessment or presentation of his subject but he himself mentions the possibility that it may yet.

The objection to this analysis is that once the biographer runs out of subjects that have long been passions of his and accepts a commission to immortalise a 'stranger', his gathering of and immersion in the raw material could be viewed as purposeful research before the fact, but he sees no difficulty: 'If the first "enthusiasm" stage of a publisher's pet project became too much like work, I would apologise and return the advance rather than proceed with a book that is bound to be flat.'

If research doesn't 'create' the book either in the beginning or in the end, what is it good for? Surprisingly, a good deal, among other things making books better and easier to read, and giving writers confidence. It is, as we shall see, not so much that the presence of proper research is such a huge benefit, but that its absence can so easily ruin a book.

THE PRACTICE OF RESEARCH

You should, for practical reasons, do the minimum of research as late as possible in your writing, cutting and rewriting cycle.

It was the research that took over my life, Father Professional writers are a dull lot, unlikely to enliven the confession box hours of even the least jaded priest. The skeleton in most of their cupboards is that they dallied on 'research' when they should have been writing, gathering 'facts' that ended up on the cutting-room floor. Don't let it happen to you. Do your research late, do it all at once, do it by letter rather than wasting time waiting for returned phone calls. When you go down to the library, have a specific list of questions, answer them and leave. Never allow yourself to waste time on ghosts: 'If only I read on another day, I might discover something startling which I might just be able to use in my book.' That's merely an excuse for not working.

Tell yourself, every time you are tempted to fly to Washington for 'research', that what happens in the author's mind is more important than what he writes in his research notebooks.

By all means haunt libraries and bookshops. I do. But do it in your allocated leisure time, not in writing time as an excuse for not writing.

What to research Consider for a moment writing a paper at college. You'd dip into a few books on the reading list to appropriate a suitable theory to organise your paper around and then you would as quickly as possible gather facts in support of the chosen theory, with a few facts against it to give you the scholarly appearance of footnotes and objectivity. The smart kid spends his time rephrasing the hoary old truths rather than doing real research because that's the cheap way to turn in a grade A fifteen-page paper for no more than a morning's work. It was, of course, a waste of good money for which, instead, one might have obtained a real education. But it is perfect training for a writer, because the writer already knows the larger things, having been educated by his enthusiasms, and has involuntarily chosen his theory by the mutation of the characters in his mind. All the writer wants are the facts in support of the theory, plus a few of the more striking opinions against for friction and colour, plus a little background for conviction or highlights. But you cannot know which parts of your concept, which of its themes, are in need of support, or whether you will need a description of the skyline of Manhattan, until you have written at least your first draft. The example is deliberately chosen: a writer who lived for years in Manhattan asked me to describe the skyline to him because from the inside he had never really seen it; when his book appeared I wondered what had happened to my description but, he said, 'A couple of drafts on she [the heroine] had to take the dachshund to the vet, so she never made it across the river and the others, who did, are too self-immersed to notice the skyline.' Half an hour each wasted on the phone on premature research, but at least better than wasting half a day driving to his nearest library and looking up picture books. On another occasion I wasted weeks reading up on geological fissures, only in the end to make my hero a mountaineer rather than a potholer

152

for no better reason than that his way of speaking once he was on the page made me think he would most likely be claustrophobic.

The Meyersco Helix (Grafton, London 1988) was a big change for Andrew McCoy, who is better known for his African adventures. But, he says, he did not make a special study of either chemistry or neurology before writing the book, in which much turns on the side-effects on the brain of a bio-war chemical accidentally released from a US military research institute.

> The encephalins in the brain, about which I learned from one of those medical novelists, Robin Cook or Michael Crichton, fascinated me, but I did nothing about it for years for lack of time until one day it gelled with another interest, the history of the abolition of the bottlewars – chemical and biological warfare, plus special knowledge about ethical drug companies from the time when I was on the board of one. This was just at the time I had agreed with Nick Austin [his publisher at Grafton] that my next book would not be set in Africa. But I didn't do any serious research beyond confirming in the library and with a neurological consultant that my pop-culture idea of how these brain-chemicals work was not diametrically opposed to the facts. For the rest, I already had a file and a bookshelf on the bottlewar-banning negotiations, and got a book from the children's library on chemistry. No point in inhibiting my invention with facts. After inventing everything and writing the penultimate draft of *The Meyersco Helix*, I asked a physician in general practice and a chemist to read it and made the amazingly few small changes they suggested so that the process was not scientifically risible.

McCoy could at this stage have gone to the library and checked his inventions against the possibilities but he feels that, with his lack of chemical training and unfamiliarity with the technical jargon of the state-of-the-art papers, he could have wasted months on what others would gladly do for him in return for a couple of evenings of enjoyable reading.

The children's library is a fruitful source for taking a quick snapshot on a subject to see if there is anything in it for you; often you can find everything you need to know about a subject instantly in books for children whereas in books for adults it is a hard slog discovering the few essential facts (which 99 per cent of the time you will not use directly in your book).

About jargon: Don't let this put you off doing serious research outside your own field if it is really necessary. A writer like Mr McCoy knows people who can help, or who can find him others who will, but even novice writers can find helpers, for instance among the students and the staff in the library. A friend who has no relevant training but whose books often require knowledge of medicine takes two hypochondriacs down to the library with him as his unofficial research assistants; they can find their way around a medical abstract a lot faster than his doctor, he says. It helps to be friendly with your doctor, with a lawyer, with a bricklayer, with as many specialists as possible, because such people can shortcut much tiresome research for you.

How much detail is required? If not very much of the research you do will show directly in your work, what you use should be highly specific. This goes beyond merely mentioning brand names, though it is as well to know, if you are writing about a small English country-town, that its solicitor is most likely to drive a Rover if he cannot afford a Mercedes or at least a Volvo, and to buy his shirts and underwear at Marks & Spencer but his suits probably and his shoes certainly somewhere more expensive.

The best method is to xerox every page on which there is a fact required and then to underline it on the xerox. The xeroxes can then be shuffled into order and discarded after use. The point about xeroxing the whole page rather than making a written note is that you can see the context and have additional facts available should you require them.

How to use research The writer does not use research to impress his authority on the reader, but simply to prevent the reader ever arriving at the point of questioning the writer's authority. There are two hazards of using too much of your research-gained knowledge. First, having it is a temptation to use it to show you have done your homework, and the result is swathes of description of very specialised matters that hold up the action long enough to wreck what started out as potentially an exciting book. Secondly, any publisher who isn't 'literary' is, in my experience, almost bound to be a technofreak; the moment they discover you have some special knowledge, their eyes and acquisitive instincts light up and out pops a demand that you positively put every jot and tittle into the book; all normal editorial standards go overboard. That's great, until the critics get hold of you and call you 'a librarian-writer' or 'an exhibitionist', but, worse, readers are not truly interested because they can see it all on television: they want to know what your characters will *do* with all this knowledge. Specialised knowledge is a devalued currency even in non-fiction, and every passing year television undercuts it further because it is so easy for an armchair warrior who has seen a single heart transplant on the box to consider he knows all about surgery. What books have is what they always had – character. Research should underpin character rather than undermine it by stealing its space.

The writer's authority None the less, you must establish the writer's authority and do it early in every book, or you will spend inordinate amounts of space explaining things that readers will take on trust from a writer who has established his authority. Your first choice should be to do it through a character and in action, because that is a hundred times more effective than doing it in description. It need not be a very large thing – just a single telling detail. As an example, in *The Zaharoff Commission* readers, already conditioned that the fiction they are being offered is very firmly based on fact, are told that the arms merchant Zaharoff, the very Pedlar of Death, prepared the salad at his own table (thirty-six solid gold settings left even after he had given thirty-six to the war effort) with his own hands when David Lloyd George and Georges Clemenceau, premiers of England and France, came to visit him in the middle of a war to ask him to end the war for them by going to Germany where there was a price on his head. Among all this astonishing detail, the almost farcical one of the salad, and Zaharoff's confession that if he had not been a steelmaster he would have wanted to be a chef, was mentioned as a very fine touch by almost every editor who worked on the book. Note that the thirty-six solid gold place-settings is dead description, but making the salad is action, and possesses the Lawrentian quickness because it reveals character.

Mister five per cent How you choose the single telling detail is a lot more problematical than knowing you should have it. My practice, now ferociously defended against all comers including my publishers, is that no more than five per cent of any special knowledge should show above the waterline of my work, fiction or non-fiction, because otherwise critical charges of technical exhibitionism follow with leaden inevitability. A more positive way of stating this is that 95 per cent of your knowledge on any subject should stay in your mind as a counterweight of confidence which will illuminate the rest of your work. For instance, this book could be ten or twenty times as thick, loaded with examples from eclectic, even indiscriminate, reading, but that would defeat the purpose of giving you a guide by which to develop, substituting instead a rule by deduction from example which would stifle your own creativity. Today, I would not put the thirty-six piece gold service in *Zaharoff* at all, contenting myself with the salad. Select your five per cent of facts to be the most striking you can find and the least likely to be known even to specialists, regardless of relative importance (remember, you can never tell your reader everything, so you may as well stick to the most interesting things), and your single most telling detail will emerge from among them in the normal process of cutting and rewriting. You won't know what it is until you get feedback on your book, probably until after publication, but our process of concentrating on character above all else virtually ensures that it will be there.

The five per cent rule has the valuable additional advantage, somewhat paradoxically, that without becoming obtrusive it impresses on the reader that you have special knowledge.

Fudging unknowns There are some things you cannot find out even in these days of Public Information Acts. In non-fiction you can tell the reader what is unknown and who prevented you from finding out – and draw appropriate conclusions. In fiction you can invent, but the ubiquity of television has made that dangerous because camera teams have been to every place possible and impassable and in the fields of abstract and applied knowledge created too many 'experts' for the comfort of lazy writers. It is better to admit, as Andrew McCoy does forthrightly in the previous chapter, that you cannot know everything. The best fudge is that your characters cannot be expected to know everything, or to care, and that their personalities shape what they observe; if they didn't see what some critic had seen in the same place or circumstance, that is probably because his vicious character or inadequate education has warped his vision. Et tu, Brutus, d'ya see the knife? A financier friend has been to a thousand barbecues on five continents but could not under torture tell you the wood burned at any of them; his brother the conservationist would ask what wood is being burned before tasting his wine or checking the meat; however, because the financier is interested in the structural uses of wood in racing yachts he can off-hand tell you the bending radius, both dry and steamed, of one-inch ash and a dozen other woods the conservationist couldn't even name. If these two were your characters, you could not put the financier in a boatyard or the conservationist at a barbeque without first knowing that these things were important to your characters and secondly finding out enough about them at least not to seem ignorant; another reason why most writers stick to their own enthusiasms at least for their main characters. If you want to know why so many otherwise liberal economists drive large cars, you first have to understand that the whole energy crisis stems from a deliberate misinterpretation of statistics in 1973 and to economists, trained to understand such matters, it was always an artificial scare; they do not feel morally bound to drive small cars when they *know* the oil is likely to last another four hundred years, half as much time again as between us and the Industrial Revolution; for practical purposes this is forever and accounts also for economists' otherwise inexplicable resistance to 'cheap' nuclear energy, which has an unpredictable afterlife and storage cost for even longer than that. It is not that economists are immoral, but that their special knowledge guides them differently. But there is no need to fudge your characters' special knowledge as far as it influences their behaviour, or not to choose an economist as a character for fear that you will miss something: it is a small matter to get yourself invited to lunch at the economics faculty of a local university and arrange to spend a few days there so that you can ask why they drive large cars and discover, sooner or later, from their general discussion, their attitudes to nuclear fuel and a great many other things.

Let others do it for you Getting people to help you is mostly a matter of the right approach. Taking my disaster with the Cambridge economists, my mistake was to let it be known from ten thousand miles away that I was coming and intended writing a novel about their main man. It would have been a lot smarter to sidle up to their pal at my publishers and get an introduction through him, to let him present me as a protégé of his prestigious firm. If you try hard enough, there is nowhere and nobody you cannot get an introduction to. Examples: for a novel about the arts in South Australia, I was introduced to the Premier of the State, Don Dunstan, by a member of his loyal opposition and given lunch and further valuable introductions. For a novel set in Alaska, State Commissioner Lisa Rudd gave me introductions to her own people, who in turn gave me introductions to specialist scholars unknown to me who lived – wait for it – twenty and fifty-five miles down the road from me. An introduction to the top men of a film company was easily come by through first arranging to handle some of their market research: I made lasting friendships – and they appointed one of their full-time writers to help me with my writing. An idea for a novel on the Anglo-Boer war led to an invitation to University College, Cork, where Jed Martin, a leading expert on colonial history, was then teaching, and being given a free run of his courses and their archives which include valuable Smuts papers; equally, through a common interest in computers with a teacher there, I am allowed the use of the closed library at the Regional Technical College. Politicians, who live on traded favours, are especially keen to make introductions for people. At the very least, ask your head librarian – librarians are surprisingly well integrated with the artistic-educational-political establishment. Big firms have public relations divisions and belong to industry bodies which, like professional associations, if approached appropriately can often arrange to put you in touch with someone both suitable and sympathetic to spend a few days with as an observer – once you're in, make a point of calling on the statisticians, whatever they are called in that industry, because they often have membership profiles and can tell you much about people inside and outside their industry.

Most libraries have a budget for buying books specially requested by members. Almost all have arrangements for borrowing books from libraries of record, and for obtaining xeroxes of rare publications or those that they simply don't stock for geographical reasons. Faraway libraries, if you write to them with return postage, will often send you relevant information and copy tapes made in local community projects to give you the colour of local people if you cannot go and see for yourself.

Sometimes writers are offered free trips or other

inducements by people who wish them to promote their region or their goods. Always make your editorial independence clear before you accept. There is also a large trade in sponsored books of which you should be aware; a sponsored book is institutionalised vanity publishing in which a company or governmental body or individual guarantees to buy an agreed number of copies of a book to resell or give away if the publisher will undertake to publish it. The work is normally offered to an established writer recommended by the publisher but there is no reason you should not try to originate something like it for yourself on your own patch, say with a local company or service board.

Under-researched writing The danger with most novices is that too much of their research will show, obtruding objectionably into the *lebensraum* of the characters, rather than that it will be under-researched. However, a lack of necessary research is easy to spot because the book reads 'thin', like an amateur stage performance in which the characters strive mightily yet fail to convince us that a wrinkled white cloth is Dunsinane Wood and what they are doing is important.

The seriously under-researched book also lacks context though at a much higher level, not so much for the missing facts as because the few given have been stretched to hide the bald spots and too much conclusion is consequent upon too few facts. A lack of confidence is also obvious, the whole reading like a series of failures of nerve, a bather repeatedly approaching the water and backing off again. The writer never gets to grip with his characters or his concept. He can't, because he didn't understand them in the first place, and that must be because he didn't know enough about them. Research won't fix this problem. The writer must start again and understand his characters before writing a new book.

There is a lesser case of under-researching, where the writer gets his characters right but fails through purest laziness to finish and fit in the sort of tertiary research with which this chapter is mainly concerned. This is extremely aggravating to editors when the writer has talent because in their hearts they want to take him on – but the publishers (who control the money) are doubtful in their heads because they know a writer who doesn't go the distance in such a simple matter right at the beginning is Forever Trouble.

The over-researched book This one, if fundamentally wrong, is no bother to spot. It reads like a thesis and the 'facts' have swamped the characters who, in consequence, in the worst cases are one hundred per cent best-quality laminated cardboard. This writer too has to return to his roots and understand his characters from scratch before starting on a new draft.

Even if the book is not fundamentally wrong, if there is merely a surplus of tertiary research tacked onto a properly characterised book, it is often almost impossible for the writer to rediscover the real story. Certainly, on a couple of occasions when I misguidedly, and under pressure from editors I had told too much at lunch who then insisted on getting all the 'hot stuff', overloaded a book with too much specialist knowledge, I had the greatest difficulty in finding the 'true' story again under all the glitter, which had meanwhile subtly changed the characters . . . Many editors seem incapable of this feat and reject a lot of good books – or what would be good books with rigorous editing – for this rather shameful non-reason. This is a very good argument for keeping dated back-up copies of your various versions of the book on disk (it is only practical on a word processor) until the book is actually in print. The remedy is to start again with the cutting and rewriting cycle, as outlined in the previous chapter, with especial reference to whether any section, paragraph or sentence is relevant to the characters and therefore to readers rather than to some jaded editor looking for a thrill. My quickest fix is to slash anything technological or in any other way special or esoteric that is not in dialogue or direct action. Afterwards you have to check the whole thing line by line to ensure your characters haven't been turned into computers or stainless steel teapots from the information overload.

The best remedy for research-failures, of whatever variety, is to know your characters and to give them preference over everything else: their actions and reactions are the only infallible guide to how much else you need to discover, to know, and to show.

9
A WRITER'S DAY AND DIFFICULTIES
BLOCKS

'WRITER'S Block' is a non-existent phenomenon that thousands truly believe they have not only observed but experienced. Blocks are to writers as Unidentified Flying Objects are to other cranks.

The exasperation displayed by old hands when confronted with the 'blocks' of aspirants arises from their knowledge that 999 out of every 1000 blocks result from the new writer's inadequate preparation or lack of discipline. The rare thousandth case derives its interest from forgivable ignorance in the face of novel circumstances; that is, the professional is patient with the blocked novice not because he believes in the block itself but because he hopes to learn something of use to his own work from the circumstances of the problem and its solution. Get it through your head early: there are no blocks that you do not create yourself. There are absolutely no psychological hardships inherent in being a writer that are not shared with a hundred other professions, so there cannot be any kind of 'psychological block', which is what is generally intended by the short form; you cannot claim special artistic dispensations – in fact, by the ground-rules we agreed at the beginning, until you are published you should not even call yourself an artist.

Proper work methods prevent blocks. However, since you cannot be expected to perfect your methods and discipline all at once, and since characterisation is the most difficult of the writing arts to master and can only be mastered with practice, problems will arise and we shall, for shorthand, call them blocks. Calm investigation of where your methods went wrong solves blocks. If the lessons practice teaches are methodically learned, one day blocks will simply no longer happen to you and, almost without noticing, you will have become a professional writer.

Meanwhile, consonant with our desire to capture as many of your words on the page with as little interruption as possible, we'll give you a headstart by showing you: first, how to avoid the most common blocks by simple routines and disciplines; secondly, how to deal with those blocks that everyone (well, perhaps not Gore Vidal, who is infuriated by the mere mention of 'blocks') must learn to overcome on their way to publication; thirdly, how to turn to advantage such blocks as arise even for professionals from time to time.

We agreed right at the beginning that perseverance is more important than talent in becoming a published writer. We agreed along the way, on examination of a good deal of circumstantial evidence, that the writer's most important attitude and belief should be that character stands above all else and is responsible for all else, the fountainhead of narrative prose. We have dealt with various theoretical and applied aspects of this thesis, taking as our key effective and affective communication between you and your reader via the reader's identification with your characters. These are all metaphysical aspects of creativity, but for creation to take place, certain mechanical protocols must be observed. Be warned: their neglect makes creating anything impossible. These rude mechanicals are the gears that make applying the rest of the advice in this book possible and you should pay them as much attention as the more readily enjoyable parts of the book.

A WRITER WRITES

The first verity is that *a writer writes*. The process of writing regularly is in itself important because book-length narratives can quite literally only be created by sitting down at your desk and writing – many, many times. Until you have sat down to write many, many times, there will be no physical corpus and therefore no creation. 'I love being a writer but hate the writing' is a joke known to every writer but they wouldn't do it, and keep doing it, if that were true. What is true is that every writer is born with a genius – unfortunately not for literature but for procrastination. They love the manifold satisfactions of writing; the bit they hate is to *sit down and start writing.*

Importance of routine As we have seen, book-length narratives are such complicated entities that their numerous tendrils can easily strangle the creative urge or its tender product. Routine is therefore important for itself, in that an ordered environment removes a layer of confusion which, on top of intrinsic creative difficulties, may be the last straw. Great books may be inspired by turmoil and upheaval but are almost always written in times of relative peace and tranquillity. Routine is also important because habits of work breed habits of thought and the mentally overbearing aspect of a book-length narrative may be mitigated by suitably ordered thinking habits. Routine presupposes both division and regularity: it helps break the most fearsomely huge project into chewable bites and holds out the promise of achievement by regular application. Routine has other advantages that you will discover for yourself. It is hard to meet a professional writer who does not hate routine – but hypocritically makes a religion of it for its rewards.

Routine specifics You *must* write regularly. That means on certain days at set times. If you have a job and busy weekends, writing on weekdays between eight and ten in the evening might be suitable. It would be better if you wrote every day of the week. If you do not have a job or studies or other regular commitments, you should, in my opinion, write about six hours every day, six or seven days a week until gradually you devise a different routine best suited to your personality or biorhythm or the section-lengths of your books.

This description of my own routine is not held up as a model – the novice should work harder than the established writer – but to demonstrate its all-inclusiveness. My workday starts when I rise about nine or ten o'clock and continues through lunch (taken at my desk) until in mid- or late-afternoon I break to take exercise, go to the library, play with my son, etc; after dinner I return to work until round about midnight. One day out of every fourteen I take off, spending half of it in the big city library, sometimes on work, sometimes on my amusement (which may yet lead to work). I do not slob in front of the television, getting up and returning to work the moment the programme I wanted to watch finishes, but always break from my work to attend to the post the moment it arrives; I also take phone calls even if I am writing, but many writers do not, their families having strict instructions to tell callers the writer will return the call. When I go to the beach or touring with visitors, my lap-top word-processor goes with me and I always get a couple of hours of work done in those periods that would otherwise be wasted just waiting for people to perform their ablutions. The upshot of this is that in ten hours a day at my desk, sometimes more, I get six hours of writing done which, on a genuinely good day, might be three thousand words of first draft and on a bad day a few hundred which are instantly chucked, ending the day with nothing more encouraging than the thought that at least tomorrow won't be wasted going down those particular dead alleys.

Since concentration lags after less than an hour, every fifty minutes you should stand up to stretch, get a cup of coffee, look out of the window. This is also a good time to do the back exercises every author should learn (the best ones are in *Back Attack* by Dr Edward Tarlov and David D'Costa, published by Little, Brown & Co) to prevent the most prevalent occupational hazard of writers – back pains. You should, for the same reason, sit in a chair with arms on which your elbows or forearms are supported as you type, with the seat set at a height which allows your feet to rest flat on the floor; lumbar support is essential and shoulder support hugely desirable.

A question often asked by novices is how much they should aim to write per session or per hour or per day and, of course, nobody can give a firm answer because it depends too much on the personality of the writer and his circumstances. On the principle that the harder you press, the higher you will achieve, you should aim for about 500 words an hour of first draft as your ultimate achievement. Start with 175 words an hour and every month, or when you achieve the target, raise it by 25 words per hour. Don't worry if you have huge ups and downs. The main thing is that, if your target for the writing session is two hours at 175 words per hour and at the end of two hours you don't have 350 words, you must carry on writing until you do have 350 words. If you have 350 words after only an hour, keep going the full two hours, striking while the iron is hot. These are individually counted words, incidentally, the only honest way to count for the writer's own satisfaction. (Word counts for publishers ignore the fact that short lines are not full and chapters do not all end on the bottom line of a page. To count words for reporting to a publisher, count the number of words in 50 *full* lines selected at random from your manuscript, divide by fifty, multiply by the number of lines per *full* page – assuming your pages all have the same number of lines, otherwise you must first determine the average number of lines per page – and multiply by the number of pages in the manuscript; do not make any allowance for shortages caused by paragraph or chapter ends. Word counts for magazines are also actual word counts, as the author does for himself.)

Some days you just know you will write nothing good. That's the good news, that you won't be disappointed by creating anything less than the King James Version. The bad news is you cannot rise up and go forth to the cinema. You must sit there, hands on the keyboard, for the full two hours, or however long your session is, and try. Write down what you dredge up, even if it is very trying indeed. This exercise is not aimed solely at avoiding a breach of the routine, though that is an important part of it, but you will be surprised how often the act of writing itself breaks you through the barrier to the point where what you write turns out to be among your best. Today I sat for almost three hours unable to start on this chapter because, quite frankly, this is a schoolmasterish part of an otherwise exciting book and I *knew* it would be dull, until it came to me that a somewhat harsher tone of voice in the introduction to warn you of the dangers of neglect would enable me, duty done, to return to the friendly, almost conspiratorial exchange of ideas with you which makes the rest of the book such a pleasure to write and, I hope, to read. If I had risen from my desk in disgust, tomorrow those three wasted hours would still have to be served, with no guarantee that the solution would come at their end, in fact less because today's strike-out would already be on the board against my confidence. Once you give up, it becomes much easier to give up the next time, and the next you won't even try. Within a week you will write nothing, and within a month your chances of ever becoming a writer will be destroyed.

It is for the same reason that you must finish every book you start, even if you know the effort will be wasted. Then, like a bull fighter or racing driver returning from a hospital bed to the scene of his humiliation and pain to fight or race again, you must immediately start another book, and for the same reason as the little boy gets back on his bike: if you don't, you will lose your nerve.

Tricks and shortcuts If you type 'The quick brown fox jumped over the lazy dog' over and over again, often the mind clears of whatever is troubling it, your characters take over, and your story swings back under full power.

It is important to start work the moment you reach your desk, otherwise a whole day, a week, a month, can slip by without you actually ever being able to say what you did with that time.

Many professional writers try always to stop in the middle of a sentence, so that they have a guideline to starting work instantly, something to pick up and run with the moment they sit down at their desks the next day. Try it: it works.

A room of one's own The writer needs to be more than a little ferocious in protecting encroachment on his writing time, partly because most people have yet to be educated that writing is work like any other. This is where a room of your own comes in handy. First, even on your first book, and even if you use a word processor, you will accumulate enough paper to make the kitchen table hazardous and a desk in the corner of the livingroom tiresome for the rest of your family. If you can't have a room of your own, a corner of a bedroom or a passage is better than the livingroom.

Because of my background in advertising and motor racing, where my office was the back of a car travelling between airports and always full of crosstalk, I can work anywhere, but even so my family know to wait at the door of my study until I look up at them. The purpose is to give me a moment to put down a marker on my line of thought instead of having it interrupted and perhaps lost for good. For the same reason someone else always answers the phone and then tells me there is a call. My wife gives five minutes or more of time-specific warning that she is serving dinner, despite the fact that we eat at a set time every evening, to allow me to finish the thought and close my word processor down in good order. Alex Hailey's morning coffee is brought to him on the minute of ten o'clock because that is when he takes a break but probably the rest are like me, slobs who are only too grateful to receive a cup of coffee at any time and slurp it absentmindedly while carrying on work. Many other writers close the door of their study and have trained their families to interrupt them only in dire emergency. ('Dammit, you're telling me what I already know. Call the fire brigade while I finish my paragraph,' one writer is supposed to have snapped, waving away smoke, when his wife burst in to report the house on fire.) One of the joys of being a writer is that you can spend more time with your family than in most other jobs, so my door is never closed. Some writers, William Goldman and John Updike for instance, have offices away from their homes that they go to during office hours, just like other professionals, perhaps precisely to avoid the situation arising where they have to close the study door.

Equipping your room The writer should have the best equipment he can afford in his workroom, starting with his chair, his typewriter or word processor, his desk lamp, and heating or air conditioning as required. The purpose is not ostentation but the reduction of distraction or delay. If you want to know, I sit in an easy chair and work on a swivelling, tilting, rolling table custom-built from surplus dental furniture.

A word processor is highly recommended because it frees so much of the time spent on the mechanical tasks of writing such as retyping. The Apple Macintosh is the professional writer's word processor computer of choice despite the fact that Apple prices are a sick joke, and software for the Mac is priced as if this joke is a licence. Cheaper word processors will do almost as much but are simply not as reliable; if your word processor goes down, you don't earn. The Mac has the advantage of the famous interface (the 'desktop') so that the writer concentrates his attention where he should, on his writing, rather than on learning the intricacies of some obtuse computer language like CP/M or DOS. The Mac is a graphic computer and therefore a natural for desktop publishing, which opens possibilities not only of selling your text on disk (you charge extra for the keying-in but note that publishers will also take discs from the cheap IBM-compatible word processors) but of laying out your own books and illustrating them yourself. For writers with weak eyes the Mac puts their text up at any size they demand, so no more peering at faint typewriting or twee little characters flickering on fuzzy screens. The word processor application of choice on the Mac is Microsoft Word, which will do everything every writer requires; if your requirements are for nothing more than straightforward narrative text, MacWrite or Microsoft Write might suffice. A writer needs only the minimum Mac, an Imagewriter II printer, and a printer cable, plus a word processor application. My own

MacPlus doesn't even have an external disk drive, never mind a hard disk; such luxuries simply are not necessary for a writer. If you can afford it and are serious about becoming a writer, I recommend the base-model Mac; if you have educational, journalistic or hospital/medical connections, you can get a big discount; sometimes bargains can be had second-hand.

Your study should also contain, close to your hand, a number of well-thumbed reference books. At a minimum you should have a good concise dictionary like the Webster or Oxford, a substantial thesaurus such as Roget's, a dictionary of quotations to suit your temperament or otherwise Bartlett's *Familiar Quotations* (Little, Brown & Co), Fowler's *Dictionary of Modern English Usage* (the cheap hardcover facsimile by Omega Books of the first edition is most amusing), Gowers' *The Complete Plain Words* (HMSO), *Writers' and Artists' Yearbook* (A & C Black, London, annually), *Novel and Short Story Writer's Market* (Writer's Digest Books, Cincinnati, annually), and the King James Version of the Bible.

Thinking time   The keenest response from professional writers to *Writing a Thriller* was evinced by its description of a writer with a perfectly regular bowel movement who spent an hour sitting on the lavatory every morning because no-one would interrupt her there and she could do the mulling every writer must: 'God, why have I never thought of that!' It had not been all that obvious to me before that thinking time was a problem for many writers, perhaps because as an habitual solitary walker it has never been difficult for me, but if it is a problem for you, you must make arrangements so that you can spend some part of every day alone with your thoughts, in exactly the same manner as you set aside writing time.

By thinking time we do not necessarily mean time spent consciously planning your book, but merely time when your thoughts are not allocated to anything else and when it is possible to relax your mind. If your characters then creep in, fine and well, do not push them out. If they do not appear, do not worry, they are working in the background of your mind. It doesn't matter if you double up your thinking time with your exercise time (though it is difficult to see how you could if you're a squash player or otherwise strenuous exerciser) or some other leisure activity – many writers walk or listen to music, a handful do carpentry (including me when the weather is really foul), one down the road here is a stamp collector, and one who lives in central London goes to a film every day but cannot tell you the plot or actors of any. All that is important is that there must be a time when your mind disengages from everyday worries. Was it Shaw or some other wise man who said we must give the idea time to creep up on us? In the same way we must give the characters time to blossom in our minds. The mutation of characters much canvassed in earlier chapters does not happen in the minds of very busy people because they are not given the space to develop.

It doesn't happen if you sit around reading someone else's book, or at least not in my experience. It doesn't happen late at night when I just want to go to sleep, but your rhythms may be different. It sometimes happens on winter mornings when I lie in, half dozing, not wanting to get out of the warm bed, and I can almost see the sparks as characters click.

A life-partner who understands that a writer is thinking when he looks out of the window is, as the comedian says, highly desirable – and if your nearest and dearest are nudgers they should be sharply discouraged.

An hour a day is plenty of thinking time as long as it is part of your daily routine, every day, every week, every month and every year. However, when you are in the planning stages of a book, or when the book goes badly, you will almost involuntarily take longer and longer walks, or whatever you do with your body in your thinking time, to give the subconscious more time to sort out your problem. Between books, my walks can grow to be very long, not because there aren't other things to do, but because the next book is germinating and experience has taught me to give it space.

172

A rule of thumb How do you draw the line between giving characters space to develop in your mind and pandering to laziness or fear of the white page? There is no instant answer. The professional does it by experience, without giving it any thought. But we know how he arrived at this experience: whether he was ready or not, whether the characters in his mind declared themselves ready or not, he sat down and wrote x number of words every day and, when they were found to be bad, chucked them out. You can't write well until you've written badly. If you write, every day, as a matter of survival, you will survive and, surviving, gain the experience to make the adjustments. This is the process described earlier of writing until you find the right tone of voice and then starting again from the beginning in that tone of voice. If you wait for the perfect inspiration, you will, no matter how talented, be a gad-fly dilettante all your life – and might not even become that, because at a certain point, unless you write them, characters start slipping away from you again and even if you then condescend to write them down they have irreversibly become caricatures. Characters must be forced into existence by writing them and then rewriting them until they are right. Not writing characters is a no-win situation.

BLOCKS AS LEARNING PROCEDURES

All blocks are created by lack of discipline or insufficient control of characterisation but the ones resulting from indiscipline are the more mechanical and so easier to deal with.

Me, I am I am The novice's common problem with an overgrown character, or a character who takes over the story to the exclusion of all else, is most often the direct result of introducing too much autobiographical material and then allowing it to run away with the writer. If it is the chief character, the book is often dead because the writer cannot persuade himself to perform the drastic surgery required. This sort of book is easily recognised because it is

173

all navel and no action, no development; in one example the whole story concerned an intellectual agonising over whether his intellect was not an insult to the workers, the sort of thing that even important politicians cannot get away with (Peter Jenkins, in the book quoted on page 141, dismisses Tony Benn scathingly for precisely this posture). Put such a book away for good and start afresh on a decidedly non-autobiographical book. But the novice who has not yet written such a book can take heed, and try to practise the self-discipline of choosing a non-autobiographical subject or, if that is impossible, keeping his own persona firmly in the background. Better a shrinking violet than a rejection slip.

Running, running nowhere man The plot that shoots off in all directions like an untended vine is commonly not a planning problem but one of characters imperfectly understood. This can usually be seen clearly by considering two propositions side by side: one, the plot doesn't work as it stands but, two, the story does not make sense whatever possible combinations of sub-plot are cut. Despite the proliferation of plots, the characters have not been given time to work themselves out completely in action. Keep cutting and writing more new material and eventually you will understand your characters well enough to put up a comprehensible complete draft. Experienced writers running into this problem often scrap the whole lot and start again from the beginning with the same characters, but there is valuable information about characterisation to be gained by the novice in doing it the hard way.

But there is a case, which readers of this book who paid the slightest attention should not meet in their own work, of the plot piled on as plot *per se*, without reference to the characters' motivations, because the author is lazy or was carried away by enthusiasm. This is clearly a case of indiscipline and, for such an apparently small breach of the rules, the consequences seem somewhat over the top. The worst examples of this are stillborn and cannot be saved because there is *nobody* there to be saved. Unfortunately these are the more common outbreaks of this disease, because the plot virus attacks the writer before the writing starts. The best but rare examples occur where there is an existing, properly characterised book on which the superfluous plot was grafted, in which case it is an easy cut-and-shut job to remove the offending excrescences by chopping sub-plots and sections wholesale.

All other blocks are the result of missing links between the character and his actions, as we have seen in the penultimate example. The reason is in each case the same, that the writer has failed to understand the character, or to give him room to develop, which comes to the same thing. Clearly differentiated examples are endless and classification controversial, but here are three of the more difficult ones that seem especially to trouble novices.

Painful perfection Hell, the editor and the reader say, real life isn't as smooth as that. Nothing extraordinary has happened in your book, but nobody believes in the action. The answer is very often characters so rigidly controlled that their small flaws are not brought into play. As a consequence the plot and the whole book has a somewhat unreal, even offensive gloss to it, with an unspecific feeling that yet there is something missing. Often, in discussion with new writers suffering this problem, one will find that they wrote so tightly to the wordage limit that there was little to cut – and no space for development. What happens with the normally written and rewritten book is that the character has space for even his flaws to develop – and then, in the normal process of rewriting, you cut some of the intermediate steps, counting on the reader to make the closures in his mind. In this way the minor character flaws make their contribution to the plot, and the portrait you're painting seems complete to the reader.

Baaaaaaad There is a special variation of this problem with bad guys. The writer creates them properly, then decides they are too lovable for his purposes and cuts them too tight, so that they come to seem almost caricatures. So what if the reader loves them? Nobody forces a writer to make moral judgements, and the best writers invariably leave them to readers. Restore the cuts; it has never hurt either Dostoevsky or Jack Higgins that they felt a keen sense of identification with their key villains.

Wishful thinking A book that works but ends before it should or ends in a manner unmotivated by the events recounted in it, is often indicative of a writer who has come too close to his characters, who loves them too much to give them their just deserts. It is true that you cannot be neutral to a character and hope to succeed with him. It is also true that if you start feeling protective of your characters you will fail. The correct attitude is that of a good foster-parent, to love each of your children deeply but resign yourself in advance to the fact that eventually they will move on. At the end of the book every character must get his just deserts, or you must justify an ending in which the reader's expectation – which you created – is disappointed. For instance, at the end of *A Season in Hell* by Jack Higgins the coldblooded killer, Jago, gets away; but Mr Higgins has not let him kill anyone except other baddies, and he has put Jago in a position to save the heroine's life several times. Now, personally, I would kill Jago, and leave the reader on a sad little note to balance his happiness at the successful conclusion for the more deserving characters, but Mr Higgins might respond sharply that I don't have his sales and that killing Jago would, after he saved the heroine's life so often, disappoint readers. It is to give you perspective on difficult questions like these that you put the book away once before cutting and rewriting and again before offering it to a publisher.

TO BEAT 'EM, FIRST JOIN 'EM

There are difficulties with characters that you will have to face even after you become a professional writer, though the pros would not call them blocks. They often arise from space allocations (misallocations in editors' eyes) the writer makes between the leading characters and the rest, or the good guys and the bad, so that someone somewhere doesn't have the space to develop; or from literary conventions that have outlived their usefulness, like the one that killers get their come-uppance, which in real life is a horselaugh. The professional solution is usually to cut these characters altogether if at all possible rather than wasting a lot of time trying to squeeze a gallon into a pint pot. The novice should do the same, consoling himself with the thought that he can save those characters for another book. In non-fiction, don't forget to remove cut characters from the index.

An artist's sensibilities If you think 'the shit endemic to a life in the arts' (William Goldman) lessens when you become a professional, stop and take stock of the opportunities offered in banking, transport and a great many other professions you are probably qualified to enter. It is important to ensure that hurt feelings do not keep you from working. The best defence against the hurts of the outside world is to mix only with those characters under your own control as you write them. The answer is to write, write, write.

10
THE BARABBAS JOURNEY
DISCOVERING AND
CULTIVATING YOUR EDITOR

F INDING a publisher is a mainly mechanical process but it is a *process* rather than an event. You should give the process quality time and attention but as little of it as possible because your business is writing – and finding a publisher is one of those secondary funtions a writer performs that, like research, can all too easily take over his life to the exclusion of his real work.

After cutting and rewriting your book, and putting it away for six months or so to gain perspective, you will read it again, and decide to make further cuts and rewrites, and perhaps to let it rest again, a process with which you should by now be very familiar. Do not be in a rush to offer your book. As we have seen, you get only one chance and that a slender one, so your book, which speaks for you, must be the very best you can do. When you are absolutely convinced you cannot improve it, then, and only then, should you offer it. Only amateurs show drafts, or partwork, or anything that isn't as good and complete as they can make it.

A methodical approach in three parts is called for.

THE BEST ADVICE IS FREE

The smart writer, convinced his book is as good as he can make it, does not in the first instance offer it to the publisher most likely to publish it or indeed, often, to any publisher. If there are regular readers in your family or among your friends, ask them to read it and tell you honestly what they think. Their opinion, even if sophisticated enough to be valuable, is usually so diffident as to be useless but it is good practice for you to attempt to elicit from them the *worst* points of the book.

Next, if you belong to a writing group, give it to them and listen politely to what they say. The bitching will be unbelievable but take detailed notes and don't respond in kind or otherwise defend your work – just listen; this is mainly practice in thickening your skin against the slings and arrows of outraged envy. (Have any of them actually finished a full-length book?) After a week or so to clear your mind, check your notes to see if there isn't a little kernel of truth in the bitching. Make the necessary changes.

Most writers move in circles in which routine and regular readers abound. Ask some of these people to read your manuscript and, never mind the flattery, tell you what they think you should do to improve it. Note the specific form of the question: not what they think is wrong with it, but what you should do to improve it, asked before they start reading. Listen, take notes, do not justify yourself, give yourself a breather and make any changes that you agree with.

Now, is there among your friends, or your family's friends, a civil servant of the old school, or an elderly school or university teacher of English – the language and grammar rather than creative writing? Ask him to work over your manuscript with a pencil and write his suggested changes on it for wrong or doubtful spelling, punctuation, grammar, construction of sentences, word choice, and obscure meanings. Don't think that a lack of attention to the formalities will not be noticed; publisher and editor will notice, and will be irritated by what one calls 'functionally illiterate manuscripts'. American editors in their tip-sheets in *Novel and Short Story Writer's Market* (Writer's Digest, Cincinnati, annually) have taken to begging authors to learn to spell! Note that you need an expert to work over your manuscript even after correcting all the obvious mis-spellings with a word processor spellchecker, as some of these editors recommend, because a spellchecker is not context-sensitive: it cannot, for instance, distinguish that 'practise' should be used where you have written 'practice'. (Please don't think I am coming the high toffee with you over this; I am in the same deplorable boat as you and whenever possible ask my friend Stuart Jay, a retired mandarin, to work over my manuscripts before giving them to publishers.) Make such changes as you agree with and certainly all the ones dealing with spelling, grammar and other such formalities where interpretation does not enter into consideration.

Next, ask yourself if you know anyone who judges narratives for a living: the editor of a local publishing house (if you live outside London or New York) even if he publishes no fiction, any publisher's reader he recommends, the books editor of a newspaper, a story editor in film or television, the producer of a local commercial or semi-commercial drama group (the amateurs are likely to be as bitchy as those in your writing group). Even a slight acquaintance or even a distant introduction, say from your head librarian, will do, because you must offer to pay this person for his time (normally only a modest sum), in return for which you can expect a written report of a page or two on your book concentrating on the coherence of the narrative and on whether the motivation of the characters is effective – the same ground that a reader's report to a publisher covers. Do not argue with his judgements because that will put him on the defensive if you have to ask for an explanation. Make the necessary changes.

There are people who offer to rewrite your manuscript for a fee. You should ask yourself, if they're such hot-shot writers, why aren't they writing their own books? Before you pay such people any money, ask them to name one author whose book they rewrote who had that book published. Anyway, unless you're going to write it yourself, why bother?

THE LITERARY AGENT

It is a fallacy that the novice cannot find an agent. He can, but most agents have been burned so often by new writers who think agents run free writing schools that the aspirant could spend more time and energy finding an agent than finding his publisher. All the same, it is worth trying since a good agent protects you from a lot of the 'shit endemic to a life in the arts' (William Goldman) and is a fount of shortcuts because he knows so much more about that side of the business than you can ever be expected to learn.

An agent is in business to represent authors who write books that can be sold. Understand that and a lot of potential grief between you and the profession of authors' representative will never happen. *Writers' and Artists' Yearbook* (A & C Black, London, annually) and *Novel and Short Story Writer's Market* (Writer's Digest Books, Cincinnati, annually) list the agents in their respective countries, together with the sort of books they specialise in. Select those you think will suit you, make a list, and write each of them in turn a letter of less than one page about your background, enclosing (unless specifically otherwise directed) only a one-page synopsis of your book (not hype, just a straightforward summary account) and a stamped self-addressed envelope for his reply. Those who do not reply obviously do not want your business. Draw a line through their entry in the reference book. Trash the letters of those who say or hint that you should return when you have sold a book to a publisher, and strike them from your reference book; they are passing the buck of their responsibility to judge saleable literature. File the letters of those who reply constructively because you might want them again, especially if they have taken the trouble to tell you something useful. James Oliver Brown, the doyen of American agents, declined to represent me and told me precisely why my book was unsaleable, a valuable lesson; when I had something he could sell, he took me on and I have been with the agent he assigned me, David Stewart Hull, ever since, longer than with all but two of my several dozen publishers.

An agent does a great deal more than just offering your manuscript to the most likely publishers and negotiating the best financial deal. A good agent tells you what is wrong with your book, and what to do to fix it. He tells you what other kind of book he thinks you could write that he can sell. He tells publishers who overstep the line where to get off. He acts as a bridge to the right people (serious publishers with deep bank accounts) and a shield against the wrong people (time-wasting would-be film-producers with rubber chequebooks).

The best agents do not charge for these services until they sell your book, when they get 15 per cent in New York and 10 per cent in London. Some agents charge a reading fee; there is no evidence that they are any better at selling books than those who do not.

If an agent does take you on, he will probably suggest changes in your book before he offers it. Make them and return a fresh manuscript.

FINDING AND KEEPING YOUR EDITOR

Note the heading. You select a publisher, but in the first instance it is an editor you must persuade to choose you and champion your work.

The editor is the contact point for the writer. Some editors still do edit books in the sense of working with writers to improve their books but more and more are acquisitions editors who want to buy books ready to go without further work because each editor is these days responsible for several times as many books than as recently as ten years ago. A publisher or publishing director is a man with a foot in the editorial camp as well as in the management camp; he normally has the final decision on which of the manuscripts the editor recommends are bought and for how much and how they are promoted, but his importance for the novice is his interest in authors as 'long-term profit centres', rather than in their individual books of which he may never read more than a few pages and in many cases none at all. The publisher is dominant personally and hierarchically and it behoves the novice to consider some beliefs common to these key executives, all of which we have discussed elsewhere, so that we need only mention them here: new authors are too much trouble and expense to establish unless the excess cost of the first book can be recouped over several books; the quality of published books moves upwards every year at an accelerated pace and the new writer must start near the top just to be certain of not being left behind; the ever-improving quality also implies that the writer must improve annually without end and new writers have no such proven staying power.

The upshot is that, unless your book is such an obvious bestseller that the publisher must contract immediately to prevent his competitors getting it, the publisher will want to keep the novice at arm's length until he proves his commitment as a writer. That is why you hear of writers whose books were rejected everywhere who make a sale, then suddenly have both books from their bottom drawers scheduled for publication as the publisher buys the same books that earlier he rejected. An introduction from someone the publisher knows, even a receptionist or copy-editor, is useful, not because it will get a bad book published, but because such people can tell the publisher that the second book in the drawer awaiting rewriting while you draft the third one is not just talk, that they have seen you grafting over a period of years. A multiple Academy Award nominee, double Oscar winner and bestselling novelist says outright that one can get to be a highly paid film writer by simply living and writing long enough in or near LA, and that his first novel, which he does not now regard highly, was published because his publisher decided he 'had become a fixture of the New York literary scene'. One hears publishers round about the age of fifty lament a time when it was possible to make a small investment in an author 'to see how he went' but that was before the international conglomerates turned mass-market publishing into a huge sudden-death play-off; by the time a publisher finishes with even 'a quality, middle-list author' (ie one not expected to be wildly popular in a mass market but there for prestige combined with regular sales and to keep the backlist honest) he will over a very few years have invested several hundred thousand dollars or pounds in that writer for advances, stock, promotion, interest and other overheads. It doesn't take many mistakes... It should be obvious that he will choose his authors carefully.

The manuscript Let's get the tedious details out of the way. Your manuscript should be typewritten or printed by daisywheel or near-letter-quality dot matrix printer, with a new ribbon, double-spaced on reasonable quality paper with a 1.5 inch margin on the left and an inch on the right. Your name and address and the number of words should be on the title page, and name and address should also be on the last page or an additional page at the back. A synopsis of one page, single-spaced, may accompany the manuscript. The paper size should be 8.5x11 inches even if you live in Europe and have to ask a printing stationer to cut it for you; this is a standard fanfold computer paper size everywhere in the world. A4 paper does not fit the manuscript boxes used in New York and Los Angeles to circulate 'properties' and manuscripts soon become very tacky. Your covering letter to the publisher should be brief, merely a paragraph offering him the manuscript and telling him you have a second book written and a third in progress; only if your personal details have a bearing on the story (if you're an airline pilot and the story is about an airliner crash) should you say so, in one sentence. You should always enclose return postage for your manuscript. Keep a copy of the manuscript; send good quality xeroxes to the publishers and keep the top copy to photocopy from again when the xerox in circulation becomes tacky. Manuscript preparation for agents is precisely the same as for publishers; never for any reason send your agent a manuscript that is not the latest version – he might offer it.

Selecting your publisher Now, with a pristine manuscript to hand, which publisher should you send it to? Take your reference book to your favourite library, together with some blank paper. Pull your ten favourite books in the subject or genre of your own book from the shelf and make a list of the publishers. If you haven't ten publishers yet, try your next ten favourite books. Now ask your librarian for the catalogues of publishers, and for trade magazines like *The Bookseller* or *Kirkus Reviews* and add the names of the ten most prolific publishers in your field to your list if they are not already there. Now consult your reference book for the preferences of publishers and arrange the publishers in the order of your preference, or by the size of their investment in your market. Copy the list out neatly so that you don't have to keep returning to the reference book every time the manuscript is declined. Offer it to each publisher in turn, from the top down. There is no reason not to offer it to two or three publishers at once but no particular reason to do it either and it would be embarrassing if all of them offered...

Unpublished books five, editors one It is unlikely that you will receive an offer from the first publisher you offer your book to, or even the tenth. You are now involved in a game of chicken. Publishers, regardless of what you may hear from unpublished writers, are avid for good new writers; the hitch is that because of the expense of establishing an author they want good new writers with nine books ready to go (preferably all at first novel, for which read insulting, advances). The game of nerves that they play is to snap up the new writer just before another publisher does. Meanwhile they hold you on a leash while · you prove your staying power even when, at this stage, there does not appear to be anything to stay for. The industry jargon is 'opening a dialogue'. It starts with a letter from an editor saying he likes your book but, what with the present state of the market, and the competitive situation, and restrictions of the distributive channels, *und so weiter* much more whining (some of it amusingly inventive), he is constrained not to offer but would you all the same let him see the second novel you mention, even if he can of course promise nothing.

The problem with this scenario, as you have no doubt already grasped, is that you cannot tell whether your first book is truly on the verge of being good enough, exactly as the man says, but just not good enough to make it, or if his publishing director said, 'Sure, the kid is good, but who needs him? If you're really that impressed, hang onto him until you can show me three like this from him.' For safety you must assume that the non-paranoid version is correct. Do not call the man a damned hypocrite and break off relations. Whatever the truth behind his protestations, he may already have put his judgement on the line for you, and will do so again if your future work does not disappoint and you play the game. Send him the second book when it is ready, and the third when that is ready. Meanwhile keep circulating all your manuscripts, and respond to other editors who open dialogues with you. It costs nothing to be polite and you are, believe me, firmly on your way to publication: dialogues are opened only with that 4 per cent of authors at any time offering manuscripts who will eventually be published. (The conclusion isn't that 96 per cent remain unpublished for all time, just not on this cycle; they must try again.)

If an editor sends you a letter which, after the usual apologetic rigmarole, says something like 'Why don't you instead try to write...', do it; drop the man a note that you're writing the book he suggested, write the book in the usual manner with pauses for perspective between creation and rewriting, and when you are certain this is *the* one send it to him. You can be sure he'll go down the line for you in his boardroom.

An editor who tells you such and such a house may be a better bet for you deserves a note of gratitude because his name is an introduction for you and he's probably weeping because he cannot publish you in his present circumstances.

Then, one day, the music will stop. A publisher will make you an offer. Editor and publisher might take you to lunch; try to listen more than you talk, and to determine the very different priorities of each. You are now a professional and should behave like one.

Contracts and subsidiary rights The novice, with or without an agent, normally tells the offering publisher politely that the offer isn't terribly exciting, the publisher ups it a little, and that's it, part of the ritual. If the writer was in dialogue with several publishing houses, a smart agent can get an auction going but most professionals would consider the budding long-term relationship between writer and editor too important to risk for a little extra on the advance.

Nor can the novice writer cut a swathe through the publisher's printed contracts, though he should resist the claim that they are carved on tablets of stone. Here are a few spitballs to look out for:

You must be paid an advance against royalties, usually split between signature and publication. However, the 'on publication' part should be paid 'on publication or within twelve months of signature, whichever is earlier'. If there is an approval clause, or any part of the payment is contingent on work yet to be done, you should add wording to the effect that 'the publisher undertakes to advise the author of acceptance, rejection or requirements for alterations within six weeks of receipt of the work or any alterations or cancel sheets to it' because if you do not, you could wait a year or longer to be paid. Cancel sheet is a trade term for a sheet of paper replacing – cancelling – one with the same number sent earlier; it carries corrections or alterations.

There must be a termination clause which comes into effect on notice from you, usually of nine months, if the publisher lets the book go out of print and does not reprint. The same clause should also state that the rights revert to you if the publisher goes bankrupt.

The geographical area the publisher is licensed to sell the book in should be clearly specified. This is usually either the American market (the States and the Philippines) or the Traditional British Market (the rest of the English-speaking world including those parts of the Empire on which the sun has set). Canada sometimes goes with the American market. The smart author can make an extra buck by selling to certain large markets, like Canada and Australia, separately but this requires local connections and is normally not possible for the novice; if you live in Canada or Australia and are in a position to make such connections, you might keep this in mind. In fiction you should not sell world rights: the publisher is entitled only to his own major market unless he has a big publishing and marketing operation in the other major market as well, and guarantees to publish the book there (his 'best efforts' with his overseas associates aren't worth hot air – you want a contractual *obligation* to publish). In non-fiction, limited-interest books and big full-colour books are often sold to a single publisher so that the cost of production can be spread across the world-markets; the rest are subject to individual negotiation. If you give the publisher the right to sell your book onwards to the other market, you should get 70 per cent of the advance and royalty which he receives from the other publisher.

Let your publisher have the translation rights: it is costly and irksome to sell them yourself, even if you know how, and he charges only a modest commission for the service.

The right to sell the reprint rights to paperback houses are also routinely given to hardcover publishers but you should get 60 per cent of the income, not half. The publisher's cut is not money wasted, but an incentive: if your first book sells well for paperbacking, that will be reflected in the publisher's attitude to you and the size of his advance for your next book. If your hardcover publisher has a paperback division, you get all the advance the paperback division pays for the reprint rights.

Some other quite valuable rights, notably condensation, digest and serialisation are also routinely licensed to your publisher of record for the simple reason that only he has the contacts to sell them. You should strike any clause claiming for the publisher 'any other right to come into existence'.

Note two important points. One, the publisher controls these rights jointly with you and should seek your approval of any sale. Two, the publisher has the right to recoup his advance to you out of the income from these rights before you are paid your share. The best publishers pay subsidiary rights income in excess of advances on receipt rather than at the annual or twice-a-year royalty accounting, but this is normally a courtesy rather than a contractual right of the author.

You should not allow the publisher broadcast, film or television rights: he rarely has expertise in selling those, and neither has the majority of agents – it is a job for which, once you are established, you must find a specialist agent.

An option clause for your next book or two books 'on the same terms' is unacceptable; 'on fair terms' is harmless because fair terms are the same as the market price, that is, the highest price obtainable elsewhere. Many professional writers consider signing option clauses intellectually dishonest because they are manifestly unenforceable, but publishers cling to them as a security blanket.

One final point: a publishing contract is a limited licence you give the publisher, in effect a franchise. Unless he honours his agreements, you have legal redress. But going to law wrecks relationships, whereas amicable compromise preserves them. On one occasion I turned in a book obviously abhorrent to the commissioning publisher and would surely have lost him by holding him to his contractual responsibility to publish, as my agent at the time advised me to do (she went that day). What actually happened is that, face to face over a few bottles of good wine, we worked out a compromise in which he commissioned two further books from me on a rollover contract (that is, on delivery of each book he would commission another one so that I could always plan two books ahead), and he was allowed to recover his advances plus, as it turned out, a profit on the unacceptable book from selling it to a paperback house; whenever another publisher asks him about me, he delivers a fulsome testimonial to my professionalism and good sense. That the writer is the principal in the author-publisher relationship is all the more reason to proceed modestly. Many of the professional bodies for writers have model contracts with which you can compare the contract your publisher sends you and you might do this from interest, as a matter of professional self-education, but publishing contracts, being of such poor legal quality that they are essentially unenforceable (how do you force an artist to deliver or a publisher to promote?), always depend more on the continuing goodwill of the parties to it than on enforcement, so don't waste time sweating the small print. If a publisher finds a condition onerous or unprofitable a year or ten after the contract is signed, he will not hesitate to ask you for relief, and you can do the same. Professional writers work on the assumption that contracts are elastically adaptable within the bounds of common sense and good-will, excepting only that they keep religiously to deadlines.

Keep writing and good luck!

NULLA DIES SINE LINEA

Not a day without writing

INDEX

Where there is a most important, or more general reference, it is listed first, with others in alphanumerical order. The names of writers mentioned in the text are not indexed unless they are quoted or paraphrased repeatedly or at length.

191